Teacher's resource

150

Literacy Hour

Lessons

YEAR 2

Contents	Page

Acknowledgements

The author and publisher would like to thank the following for permission to reproduce material in this book:

'Mog and the Vee Ee Tee' by Judith Kerr reproduced with the permission of HarperCollins Publishers Ltd. 'Mr Gumpy's Outing' by John Burningham reproduced with the permission of Random House, London. 'Night Time Fright Time' by John Foster (from 'You Little Monkey') reproduced with the permission of the author. 'After Dark' from 'Tea in the Sugar Bowl, Potato in My Shoe' text © Michael Rosen, illustrated by Quentin Blake. Reproduced by permission of the publisher Walker Books Ltd., London. 'Morning' by Grace Nichols (from 'Give Yourself a Hug') reproduced with the permission of Curtis Brown Limited. 'I'm Just Going Out for a Moment' by Michael Rosen (from 'Poems Not to Be Missed' selected by Susan Hill) reproduced with the permission of Heinemann Books. 'My Sweet' by Richard Brown (from 'A Lick of the Spoon') published by Cambridge University Press and reproduced with the permission of the author. 'On the Ning Nang Nong' by Spike Milligan (from 'Silly Verse for Kids') reproduced with the permission of Spike Milligan Productions. 'Because of Figs' by Ann Cameron (from 'The Julian Stories') reproduced with the permission of Ellen Levine Literary Agency, New York. 'Upstairs and Upstairs' by Jan Mark (from 'Twig Thing') reproduced with the permission of David Higham Associates. 'The King with Dirty Feet' retold by Robert Clayton (from 'The King With Dirty Feet and Other Stories' selected by Mary Medlicott) reproduced with the permission of Kingfisher Publications.

Every effort has been made to trace and acknowledge ownership of copyright material but if any have been inadvertently overlooked, the publisher will be pleased to make the necessary alterations at the first opportunity.

First published 2001
exclusively for WHSmith by

Hodder & Stoughton Educational,
a division of Hodder Headline Ltd.
338 Euston Road
London NW1 3BH

Text and illustrations © Hodder & Stoughton Educational
2001

A CIP record for this book is available from the British
Library.

Authors: Peta Lloyd and Louise Winship
Series editor: Gill Matthews

ISBN 0340 78997 2

Typeset by Fakenham Photosetting
Printed and bound in Spain by Graphycems

How to use this book

Each term is divided into ten weekly themes, organised as follows:

• Objectives for the week
These are taken from the National Literacy Strategy Framework for teaching and form the basis of medium term planning for text, sentence and word level work.

• Resources
A list of the materials that are needed to teach the theme. Some themes are generic and a range of texts could be used while others are written around suggested texts.
Where necessary, preparation that can be carried out in advance is highlighted.

• Assessment
This is an outline of broad assessment objectives, recognising that many teachers already have detailed recording and assessment procedures in place in their schools.

• Lesson outlines
Each lesson is divided into the following sections:

Whole class
This section contains suggestions for whole class shared reading or writing activities. The final outcome of most themes is a completed piece of written work. The whole class teaching aims to guide children through the objectives in order to achieve this.

Group and independent work
This section contains ideas for group work, whether guided by you or another adult, or independent work. The suggested activity may be the task that you focus on with a group. How these activities are used will depend on your particular organisation.

Differentiation
Most lessons are accompanied by differentiated activities for high and low attainers and suggestions for where it would be suitable for children to work in mixed ability pairs.

Whole class
The final section of each lesson gives ideas for a plenary session, including:
- activities which revisit key learning objectives;
- feedback from children, either individuals, pairs or in some cases the whole class, on the work they have been doing;
- feedback from children on a partner's work;
- preparation for the next day's lesson
- class evaluation of a lesson or a theme of work.

• Photocopiable masters (copymasters)
Most themes are accompanied by photocopiable masters for use in whole class and group time. These are not work sheets to practise taught skills, but are closely linked to the content of the lesson. Many can be used as frames for collecting discussed ideas or for shared writing in whole class sessions, as well as by the children in group or independent work.

• Homework
Each theme is accompanied by a photocopiable homework sheet which explains to parents or guardians what the children have been doing in literacy work for that particular week. This is followed by a task that can be carried out by the child.

Throughout the themes the development of reading and writing skills are linked closely. Themes or blocks of themes start with an emphasis on the teaching of reading through shared reading, use the reading as a stimulus or model for shared writing and suggest ideas for children's writing based on the shared work that has been carried out.

Shared reading

The different reading organisations covered include:
- teacher reading to the children;
- children reading with the teacher;
- class reading without the teacher joining in;
- a group reading to the rest of the class;
- individual children reading to the class.

Shared writing

This book suggests activities whereby teachers model writing, provide a scaffold to support children in their writing and teach writing over a sequence of lessons. Children's writing should be used in shared sessions as a means of encouraging the early stages of drafting and improving writing.

Word level work

In order to ensure the appropriate emphasis and

How to use this book

focus it is often better to introduce word level work separately from text level work. Teachers will lead children in using their word level skills within shared reading and writing.

• Phonics

Phonic work should be used to support reading and children should be encouraged to see links between phonic activities, and shared and guided reading activities. Phonic work should also be incorporated into shared writing activities. Children can be encouraged to use word lists generated in phonic work to help with spellings. Many children find a class-made 'long vowel' dictionary a useful writing support.

• Word recognition, graphic knowledge and spelling

Word walls, lists and cards are ways of displaying and drawing children's attention to words that need to become part of their sight vocabulary. Recognition and practice of these words can be incorporated into shared and guided work.

• Handwriting

Most schools have adopted a particular handwriting scheme and many teachers have taken the practising of handwriting out of the Literacy Hour. However, modelled and shared writing provide good opportunities to demonstrate handwriting.

Teaching and learning strategies

A range of teaching techniques are suggested to make lessons interactive and ensure the involvement of all children. These include:

• Use of the 'time out' strategy during whole class sessions where pairs or small groups of children are given short periods of time to discuss a question, think of an appropriate word or compose a sentence.
• Pairing children during group work to encourage discussion and develop collaborative skills.
• Feedback from the class when sitting in a circle.
• Use of small whiteboards. These can be purchased from suppliers or made by laminating card and used with appropriate pens.
• Many teachers now make use of large white boards for shared writing and related activities. Large sheets of sugar paper may be more appropriate for some activities as they can be:
  – displayed as a model for writing;

  – used as part of a 'work in progress' display;
  – referred to as a memory jogger;
  – re-read as a familiar text, which can be particularly useful for low attaining children.

Speaking and listening

A range of suggestions for the inclusion of speaking and listening are included such as:

• organising a range of audiences for reading and for the sharing of written work;
• encouraging children to listen to each other in discussion about aspects of texts;
• asking children to respond to a range of questions, to give opinions and share ideas;
• making use of drama techniques such as 'hotseating', where some children are encouraged to take on a role and others to ask questions, during whole class work.

ICT

The amount of use made of ICT depends on many factors such as the hardware available and teachers' confidence in using it. A range of suggestions for its use are offered.

Word processing

The majority of writing activities that are carried out with paper and pencil can be fulfilled using a word processing package. Children's lack of word processing skills often makes tasks such as producing a final copy of a piece of written work laborious and time consuming. However, opportunities for word processing can be organised through tasks such as creating captions, labels, book titles and headings.

The Internet

The Internet may be used to find information relating to fiction and non-fiction work.

E-mail

There are a growing number of local, national and international projects making use of the school e-mail address to develop links with other groups and share information and ideas.

Word and sentence level activities

There are a growing number of programs available to support spelling development and the learning of certain grammatical structures.

Each term is divided into ten weekly themes, organised as follows:

• Objectives for the week

These are taken from the National Literacy Strategy Framework for teaching and form the basis of medium term planning for text, sentence and word level work.

• Resources

A list of the materials that are needed to teach the theme. Some themes are generic and a range of texts could be used while others are written around suggested texts.

Where necessary, preparation that can be carried out in advance is highlighted.

• Assessment

This is an outline of broad assessment objectives, recognising that many teachers already have detailed recording and assessment procedures in place in their schools.

• Lesson outlines

Each lesson is divided into the following sections:

Whole class

This section contains suggestions for whole class shared reading or writing activities. The final outcome of most themes is a completed piece of written work. The whole class teaching aims to guide children through the objectives in order to achieve this.

Group and independent work

This section contains ideas for group work, whether guided by you or another adult, or independent work. The suggested activity may be the task that you focus on with a group. How these activities are used will depend on your particular organisation.

Differentiation

Most lessons are accompanied by differentiated activities for high and low attainers and suggestions for where it would be suitable for children to work in mixed ability pairs.

Whole class

The final section of each lesson gives ideas for a plenary session, including:

- activities which revisit key learning objectives;
- feedback from children, either individuals, pairs or in some cases the whole class, on the work they have been doing;
- feedback from children on a partner's work;
- preparation for the next day's lesson
- class evaluation of a lesson or a theme of work.

• Photocopiable masters (copymasters)

Most themes are accompanied by photocopiable masters for use in whole class and group time. These are not work sheets to practise taught skills, but are closely linked to the content of the lesson. Many can be used as frames for collecting discussed ideas or for shared writing in whole class sessions, as well as by the children in group or independent work.

• Homework

Each theme is accompanied by a photocopiable homework sheet which explains to parents or guardians what the children have been doing in literacy work for that particular week. This is followed by a task that can be carried out by the child.

Throughout the themes the development of reading and writing skills are linked closely. Themes or blocks of themes start with an emphasis on the teaching of reading through shared reading, use the reading as a stimulus or model for shared writing and suggest ideas for children's writing based on the shared work that has been carried out.

Shared reading

The different reading organisations covered include:
- teacher reading to the children;
- children reading with the teacher;
- class reading without the teacher joining in;
- a group reading to the rest of the class;
- individual children reading to the class.

Shared writing

This book suggests activities whereby teachers model writing, provide a scaffold to support children in their writing and teach writing over a sequence of lessons. Children's writing should be used in shared sessions as a means of encouraging the early stages of drafting and improving writing.

Word level work

In order to ensure the appropriate emphasis and

How to use this book

focus it is often better to introduce word level work separately from text level work. Teachers will lead children in using their word level skills within shared reading and writing.

• Phonics
Phonic work should be used to support reading and children should be encouraged to see links between phonic activities, and shared and guided reading activities. Phonic work should also be incorporated into shared writing activities. Children can be encouraged to use word lists generated in phonic work to help with spellings. Many children find a class-made 'long vowel' dictionary a useful writing support.

• Word recognition, graphic knowledge and spelling
Word walls, lists and cards are ways of displaying and drawing children's attention to words that need to become part of their sight vocabulary. Recognition and practice of these words can be incorporated into shared and guided work.

• Handwriting
Most schools have adopted a particular handwriting scheme and many teachers have taken the practising of handwriting out of the Literacy Hour. However, modelled and shared writing provide good opportunities to demonstrate handwriting.

Teaching and learning strategies

A range of teaching techniques are suggested to make lessons interactive and ensure the involvement of all children. These include:

- Use of the 'time out' strategy during whole class sessions where pairs or small groups of children are given short periods of time to discuss a question, think of an appropriate word or compose a sentence.
- Pairing children during group work to encourage discussion and develop collaborative skills.
- Feedback from the class when sitting in a circle.
- Use of small whiteboards. These can be purchased from suppliers or made by laminating card and used with appropriate pens.
- Many teachers now make use of large white boards for shared writing and related activities. Large sheets of sugar paper may be more appropriate for some activities as they can be:
  - displayed as a model for writing;
  - used as part of a 'work in progress' display;
  - referred to as a memory jogger;
  - re-read as a familiar text, which can be particularly useful for low attaining children.

Speaking and listening

A range of suggestions for the inclusion of speaking and listening are included such as:

- organising a range of audiences for reading and for the sharing of written work;
- encouraging children to listen to each other in discussion about aspects of texts;
- asking children to respond to a range of questions, to give opinions and share ideas;
- making use of drama techniques such as 'hotseating', where some children are encouraged to take on a role and others to ask questions, during whole class work.

ICT

The amount of use made of ICT depends on many factors such as the hardware available and teachers' confidence in using it. A range of suggestions for its use are offered.

Word processing
The majority of writing activities that are carried out with paper and pencil can be fulfilled using a word processing package. Children's lack of word processing skills often makes tasks such as producing a final copy of a piece of written work laborious and time consuming. However, opportunities for word processing can be organised through tasks such as creating captions, labels, book titles and headings.

The Internet
The Internet may be used to find information relating to fiction and non-fiction work.

E-mail
There are a growing number of local, national and international projects making use of the school e-mail address to develop links with other groups and share information and ideas.

Word and sentence level activities
There are a growing number of programs available to support spelling development and the learning of certain grammatical structures.

Autumn term

	Theme	Objectives: children will be taught to:
1	Stories with familiar settings	Be aware of the difference between spoken and written language through comparing oral recounts with text. Make use of formal story elements in re-telling. Understand time and sequential relationships in stories, i.e. what happened when. Identify reasons for events in stories linked to plot. Discuss familiar story themes and link to their own experiences. Use word endings, e.g. ed (past tense), ing (present tense) to support reading and spelling.
2	Stories with familiar settings	Understand time and sequential relationships in stories, i.e. what happened when. Identify reasons for events in stories linked to plot and link them to their own experiences. Discuss familiar story themes. Use story structure to write about their own experience in the same or similar form. Use the word ending ed to support their reading and spelling.
3	Stories with familiar settings	Be aware of the difference between spoken and written language through comparing oral recounts with text. Make use of formal story elements in re-telling. Understand time and sequential relationships in stories, i.e. what happened when. Identify and discuss reasons for events in stories linked to plot. Discuss familiar story themes and link them to their own experiences. Recognise and take account of commas and exclamation marks when reading aloud with appropriate expression. Secure identification, spelling and reading of long vowel digraphs in simple words from Year 1 Term 3 (ee/ea).
4	Stories with familiar settings	Discuss familiar story themes and link them to their own experiences. Use story structure to write about their own experience in the same or similar form. Use the language of time to structure a sequence of events. Re-read their own writing for sense and punctuation.
5	Stories with familiar settings	Be aware of the difference between spoken and written language through comparing oral recounts with text. Make use of formal story elements in re-telling. Understand time and sequential relationships in stories, i.e. what happened next. Use boxes and arrows as simple organisational devices to indicate sequence. Use the word ending ed (past tense) to support reading and spelling.
6	Stories with familiar settings	Use a story structure to write another story. Re-read their own writing for sense and punctuation.
7	Poems with familiar settings	Learn, re-read and recite favourite poems, taking account of punctuation and to comment on aspects such as word combinations, sound patterns (rhymes, rhythms, alliteration) and forms of presentation. Collect and categorise poems to build class anthologies. Use simple poetry structures and substitute their own ideas or write new lines. Recognise and take account of commas and exclamation marks when reading aloud with appropriate expression. Revise knowledge about uses of capitalisation for titles and emphasis. Build individual collections of significant words.
8	Poems with familiar settings	Collect and categorise poems to build class anthologies. Through shared and guided writing apply phonological and graphic knowledge and sight vocabulary to spell words accurately. Use simple poetry structures and substitute their own ideas.
9	Instructions	Read simple written instructions in the classroom (recipes, plans, instructions for constructing something). Note key structural features. Write simple instructions. Use models from reading to organise instructions sequentially. Use diagrams in instructions. Use appropriate register in written instructions. Find examples in fiction and non-fiction of words and phrases that link sentences. Use a variety of simple organisational devices to indicate sequences and relationships.
10	Instructions	Read simple written instructions in the classroom (recipes, plans, instructions for constructing something). Note key structural features. Write simple instructions. Use models from reading to organise instructions sequentially. Use diagrams in instructions. Use appropriate register in written instructions. Find examples in fiction and non-fiction of words and phrases that link sentences.

Summary of objectives

Spring term

	Theme	Objectives: children will be taught to:
1	Traditional stories	Identify and describe characters. Write simple descriptions of characters. Be aware of the need for grammatical agreement in speech and writing, matching verbs to nouns/pronouns correctly. Use commas to separate items in a list. Build collections of significant words.
2	Traditional stories	Reinforce and apply word level skills through shared and guided reading. Discuss story settings, locate key words and phrases in text and consider how different settings influence events and behaviour. Identify and describe characters, expressing their own views and using words and phrases from the text. Prepare and re-tell stories individually through role-play in groups, using dialogue and narrative from the text. Write character profiles.
3	Traditional stories	Through shared and guided writing apply phonological and graphic knowledge and sight vocabulary to spell words accurately. Use story settings from reading in their own writing. Re-read their own writing to check for grammatical sense and accuracy, identifying errors and suggesting alternative constructions. Be aware of the need for grammatical agreement in speech and writing, matching verbs to nouns/pronouns correctly.
4	Traditional stories from other cultures	Predict incidents from the text. Identify and describe characters, using words and phrases from the text. Write character profiles using key words and phrases that describe, or are spoken by, characters in the text. Identify speech marks in reading, understand their purpose and use the term correctly. Use antonyms, collect and discuss differences of meaning and their spellings.
5	Traditional stories from other cultures	Discuss story settings and compare differences. Locate key words and phrases in the text. Use story settings from reading. Secure the use of simple sentences in their own writing. Build individual collections of significant words.
6	Traditional stories from other cultures	Use story settings from reading to write a different story in the same setting. Re-read their own writing to check for grammatical sense and accuracy, identifying errors and suggesting alternative constructions. Use new words from reading.
7	Poems with predictable and patterned language	Identify and discuss patterns in rhythm and rhyme in different poems. Comment on and recognise when the reading aloud of a poem makes sense and is effective. Identify and discuss favourite poems, referring to the language of a poem. Use structures from poems as a basis for writing by extending and substituting elements. Read aloud with intonation and expression appropriate to the grammar and punctuation. Split familiar oral and written compound words into their component parts. Discriminate orally syllables in multi-syllabic words from reading, extend to written forms and note syllable boundary in speech and writing.
8	Poems with predictable and patterned language	Read poems aloud. Identify and discuss patterns of rhythm. Comment on and recognise when the reading aloud of a poem makes sense and is effective. Use structures from poems as a basis for writing by substituting elements and inventing their own lines.
9	Explanations	Read flow charts and cyclical diagrams which explain a process. Produce simple flow charts or diagrams that explain a process.
10	Dictionaries and other alphabetically ordered texts	Use dictionaries to locate words by using the initial letter. Know that dictionaries give definitions and explanations, discuss what definitions are and explore some simple definitions in dictionaries. Use other alphabetically order book and discuss how they are used.

Summer term

	Theme	Objectives: children will be taught to:
1	Different stories by the same author.	Compare books by the same author, examining settings, characters and themes. Evaluate giving reasons. Read about authors from information on book covers. Become aware of authorship and publication. Write simple evaluations of books read and discussed giving reasons.
2	Different stories by the same author.	Compare books by the same author, examining settings, characters and themes. Evaluate giving reasons. Read about authors from information on book covers. Become aware of authorship and publication. Write simple evaluations of books read and discussed giving reasons.
3	Different stories by the same author.	Compare books by the same author, examining settings, characters and themes. Evaluate giving reasons. Read about authors from information on book covers. Become aware of authorship and publication. Write simple evaluations of books read and discussed giving reasons.
4	Texts with language play: riddles	Read and collect examples of riddles. Use riddles as a structure for children to write their own by adaptation, selecting words with care. Turn statements into questions. Learn a range of 'wh' words typically used to open questions: what, when, where, who, and add question marks.
5	Texts with language play: humorous verse	Discuss the meanings of words and phrases that create humour. Use humorous verse as a structure for children to write their own adaptations. Read text aloud with intonation and expression appropriate to the grammar and punctuation. Use synonyms and other alternative words/phrases that express the same or similar meanings.
6	Extended stories	Notice the difference between spoken and written forms through re-telling known stories. Compare oral versions with the written text. Read about authors from information on book covers. Compare books by different authors on similar themes. Recognise the need for grammatical agreement, matching verbs to nouns/pronouns and using simple gender forms.
7	Extended stories	Write sustained stories, using their knowledge of story elements, narrative, setting, characterisation, dialogue and the language of story
8	Extended stories	Write sustained stories, using their knowledge of story elements. Read aloud with intonation and expression appropriate to the grammar and punctuation.
9	Information texts	Understand the distinction between fact and fiction. Use the terms 'fact', 'fiction' and 'non-fiction' appropriately. Use a contents page and index to find their way about a text. Scan a text to find specific sections. Skim read the title, contents page, illustrations, chapter and sub headings to speculate what a book might be about. Evaluate the usefulness of a text for its purpose.
10	Information texts	Pose questions and record them in writing before reading a non-fiction text. Find answers. Make simple notes from non-fiction texts, *e.g. key words and phrases, page references, headings*, to use in subsequent writing. Write non-fiction texts, using texts read as models for their own writing. Learn a range of 'wh' words typically used to open questions and add question marks.

Objectives

Text level

- 3 To be aware of the difference between spoken and written language through comparing oral recounts with text and to make use of formal story elements in re-telling;
- 4 To understand time and sequential relationships in stories, i.e what happened when;
- 5 To identify reasons for events in stories linked to plot;
- 6 To discuss familiar story themes and link to own experiences.

Word level

- 7 To use word endings, e.g. 'ed' (past tense), 'ing' (present tense), to support reading and spelling.

Resources

'This is the Bear' by Sarah Hayes and Helen Craig. Copymaster 1, Copymaster 2. Homework 1

Resource preparation

After the first two or three pages, cover up the last word in the rhyming pair, allowing the children to predict the word.

Enlarge four pictures from the text for the children to sequence.

Prepare a sheet for the children to sequence with smaller copies of these pictures in the wrong order. Set up a 'washing line' in the classroom for picture sequencing.

Assessment

At the end of this theme is the pupil able to:
- re-tell a simple story in the correct order;
- identify differences between spoken and written language;
- use word endings 'ing', 'ed' and 's' correctly in their writing;
- identify reasons for events in stories linked to plot?

Lesson 1

Whole class

Begin by looking at the front cover of the text. Ask the children who they think the main characters in the story will be. What do they think the relationship between the boy and the bear is like? How do they think the dog feels? Ask the children to predict the key events in the story from looking at the front cover of the book. After the first two pages, cover up the second rhyming word in each pair of rhyming words for the children to predict. Read the text with the children, stopping after the second page. Ask the children to identify patterns in the text, *e.g. each page begins with 'this is', it is a rhyming text.* Finish reading the text together. Put the four enlarged pictures from the text on the washing line in the wrong order. Ask the children if anyone can sequence the pictures into the correct order. Write one or two sentences to accompany each picture in the style of the book, i.e each sentence beginning with 'This is…'.

Group and independent work

Give each child a sheet with small versions of the pictures on the washing line. Ask the children to sequence the pictures in the correct order, adding the text underneath the pictures.

Differentiation

Low Attainers – Give children the pictures, and the text which accompanies the pictures, to sequence.
High Attainers – Ask children to add two or more pieces of text between two of the pictures to fill in some of the gaps in the story.

Whole class

Give some of the children the four enlarged pictures to hold and ask them to put themselves in the correct order. Ask the children if anyone would like to stand with the children holding the pictures and read the text that accompanies that particular picture.

Lesson 2

Whole class

Ask children to re-tell the story. The re-telling can be the children's own words and doesn't have to be told in the style of the text. Ask the children to compare the way that the story has been re-told with the way the book is actually written. What were the key differences? Tell the children to identify the main characters in the story. Focus on the character of the dog. Ask the children to tell you how the dog felt at the beginning of the story. How did he feel when the boy found out the bear was missing? How did the dog feel at the end of the story? Repeat this with the bear and the boy. Prepare a picture of the bear, the dog and the boy. Tell the children that they are going to add thought bubbles to each character to show how they felt at each stage. Model how to give each character a thought bubble. Ask the children to describe how each character felt at the beginning of the story, *e.g. I felt jealous of the bear.* Write the children's ideas into the thought bubbles.

Group and independent work

Give the children pictures of the boy, the bear and the dog. Tell the children to stick a picture of each character into their books and give them a thought bubble showing their feelings at the beginning of the story. Repeat this for the middle and the end.

Differentiation

Low Attainers – Ask the group to brainstorm words to describe each character and write them by the pictures.
High Attainers – Ask this group to think about reasons for the characters' feelings.

Whole class

Have a picture of each of the characters and three pieces of paper with 'beginning', 'middle' and 'end' written on them. Ask for a volunteer to choose a character and a time in the story. Ask that child to describe that character's feelings at that particular time in the story and give reasons for their feelings.

Lesson 3

Whole class

Ask the children to think about the character of the dog and his feelings towards the bear at the beginning of the story. Ask the children if anyone has ever felt jealous of someone. Choose some children to recount their experiences to the rest of the class. Put the children into pairs and ask them to tell their partner about a time when they have been jealous of someone. Ask the children to tell their partner who it was, what they were jealous of and what they did about their jealousy. Ask some of the children to re-tell their partner's story to the rest of the class. Construct a class writing frame to support the children when writing their account of feeling jealous. You may wish to base this frame on Copymaster 1. Begin to complete the writing frame with the children using one of their stories from earlier in the session.

Group and independent work

Ask the children to use the writing frame to write their account of a time when they have felt jealous. If anyone is unable to think of ideas they can write as if they were the dog in the story. You may wish to give some children a copy of Copymaster 1 to use as a structure for this work.

Differentiation

Low Attainers – Ask children to discuss their feelings of jealousy in a group with adult support if appropriate. Ask them to draw a picture of their experience adding a simple sentence, e.g. *I felt jealous when ….*
High Attainers – Encourage children to extend their work, thinking carefully about their choice of adjectives to describe their feelings. Ask children to focus on giving reasons for their feelings and actions.

Whole class

Ask some children to tell their stories to the rest of the class. Focus on whether the children have given the reader sufficient detail and any effective use of adjectives.

Lesson 4

Whole class

Look at the text again with the children, focusing on the use of speech bubbles in the story. Ask the children if they can tell you what the speech bubbles add to the story. Tell the children a simple, fictional or true story about a time when you have felt jealous. Discuss the events in your story with the children and the reasons why you were feeling jealous. Using an enlarged version of Copymaster 2, ask the children to help you to divide your story into four sections. Write four sentences, one underneath each box to re-tell your story. Read the writing under the first box with the children and ask them to suggest an idea for an illustration to go into the first box. Draw the picture that the children have suggested in the first box. Put the children into pairs and give each pair a whiteboard. Ask the pairs to think of something that one of the characters in the story might be saying or thinking, which could go into a thought or speech bubble for that character. Ask the pairs to share their ideas with the rest of the class. Choose one of the ideas to write into a thought or speech bubble for one of the characters.

Group and independent work

Give each child a copy of Copymaster 2. Ask the children to use your story to scribe the four sentences under the boxes. Ask the children to finish adding the pictures to the boxes and give one character a speech or thought bubble that describes their feelings at that time.

Differentiation

Low Attainers – Ask children to draw one picture that tells the story of a time when they felt jealous. The children can add speech or thought bubbles.
High Attainers – Ask children to divide their own account from the previous session into four sections and write four of their own sentences under the boxes. Ask the children to add their illustrations and speech or thought bubbles to their work.

Whole class

Encourage children to imagine that they are characters from your story. Ask them to think of something that a character might say to describe his or her feelings at a particular time in the story. Ask the children to say their ideas as if they were that character. Can the rest of the class guess which character from the story they are?

Lesson 5

Whole class

Read the big book with the children. Ask the children to show you a sign every time they identify a word which ends in 'ed'. Make a class list of these words. Ask the children to read the words without the suffix 'ed' added, e.g. *pushed = push*. Give pairs of children a whiteboard. Give the children a selection of words which have the suffix 'ed' added. Ask them to write the word without the suffix onto their board. Give the children a few more words where the suffix has not been added. Ask the children to add 'ed'. Explain to the children that the story is being told about events that have already happened, i.e. it has happened in the past. Ask the children if they can change each of the words to the present, as if it was happening now. Begin each sentence with 'I am', e.g. *'I am pushing him'*. Draw attention to the addition of 'ing', when the action is happening in the present.

Group and independent work

Ask the children to put the words in the list into sentences, adding the suffix 'ed' or 'ing'.

Differentiation

Low Attainers – Using flash cards, ask this group to add 'ing' to four or five words.
High Attainers – Ask the children to think of their own words with 'ed' or 'ing' and put these into sentences.

Whole class

Go through each of the words with the children and ask some of the children to read their sentences.

Objectives

Text level

- 4 To understand time and sequential relationships in stories, i.e. what happened when;
- 5 To identify reasons for events in stories, linked to plot and link to own experiences;
- 6 To discuss familiar story themes;
- 10 To use story structure to write about own experience in same/similar form.

Word level

- 7 To use the word ending 'ed' to support their reading and spelling.

Resources

'This is the Bear and the Scary Night' written by Sarah Hayes and Helen Craig (big book version if possible).

Copymaster 3, Copymaster 4. Homework 2.

Resource preparation

Photocopy Copymaster 3, cut it up and put a set of words into an envelope for the children to sort (enough for one envelope for each pair of children).

Assessment

At the end of this theme is the pupil able to:

- identify the reasons for events in a story and link this to their own experiences;
- use a given story structure to write in the same or similar form;
- use the word ending 'ed' to support their reading and spelling?

Lesson 1

Whole class

Introduce the text to the children. Ask whether they recognise the main character from the story. Tell the children that the book comes from the same series as 'This is the Bear' and involves the same characters. Look at the front cover with the children. Ask whether the illustration on the front cover tells them how the bear is feeling and what the text may be about. Read the text with the children and discuss the story, compared to their predictions from the front cover.

Ask the children to locate any words in the text which have the suffix 'ed'. Add these words to the class lists from the previous week. Look at all the words collected so far. Ask the children if they can start to see any spelling rules for adding 'ed' to a word, *e.g. if the word already ends with an 'e' you only need to add the 'd'*. Put the children into pairs and give each pair a whiteboard. Test a few of the rules with the children by giving them words to which you can add the suffix 'ed'.

Group and independent work

Give pairs of children an envelope containing a set of words from Copymaster 3. Ask the children to sort them into columns according to which spelling rule applies to that word when adding 'ed'. Tell children to stick their lists of words onto a sheet of paper. Ask the children to add their own words to each column when they have finished.

Differentiation

Low Attainers – This group can be paired with more able children for the word sorting investigation.

High Attainers – Ask children to put some of the words into sentences, reinforcing the use of past tense.

Whole class

Ask the children to help you to sort the list of words on Copymaster 3, reinforcing the spelling rules for adding 'ed' to a word. Make a list of rules to display in the classroom.

Lesson 2

Whole class

Re-read the text with the children. Recap on the story of 'This is the Bear' from the previous week. Can the children remember the theme of the book? Ask the children to identify the theme of this week's book. Remind the children of the picture on the front cover. How can we tell how the bear is feeling from this picture? Ask a child to come out to the front and take on the role of the bear in this story. The rest of the class can ask the bear questions relating to the plot. When all of the questions have been answered, ask the children to tell you what they have found out about the bear. It may be helpful to list their responses. Tell the children that they are going to re-tell the story from the bear's point of view. Through shared writing, begin the piece of writing with the children, focusing on the language used when writing in the first person.

Group and independent work

Ask the children to tell the story to a partner of the night that the bear got lost from the bear's point of view. You may wish to ask some children to focus on one part of the story only.

Differentiation

Low Attainers – These children can re-tell the story orally from the bear's point of view. They could record their stories.

High Attainers – Ask these children to re-tell the whole story. Encourage this group to think carefully about their choice of adjectives to describe feelings and places in the story.

Whole class

Children sit in a circle. Ask the children to re-tell parts of the story in the correct order as if they were the bear. Focus on use of language when the story is told in the first person.

Lesson 3

Whole class

Ask the children if anyone in the class has ever been lost. Choose one or two children to tell their stories to the rest of the class. In pairs, ask children to tell each other about a time when they have been lost or felt frightened. Encourage the child listening to the story to ask their partner questions about their story and their feelings. Ask one pair to tell the rest of the class their partner's experiences of feeling lost or frightened. Discuss similarities between their story and the bear's story. Choose one of the children's stories to use as an example and model how to write an account of feeling lost or frightened. Focus on the use of adjectives to describe feelings and places to make the writing more interesting. Give the children a sentence starter for their writing, *e.g. Let me tell you about the time when ...* Encourage the children to tell their account like a story; encourage awareness of the audience. You may wish to construct a writing frame to help children structure their writing.

Group and independent work

Ask the children to write an account of a time they have been lost or frightened. Encourage the children to write their account as if they were writing a story.

Differentiation

Low Attainers – This group can record their story pictorially, adding sentences or captions to the pictures.

High Attainers – Ask children to swap their work with a friend halfway through their story. Encourage the children to suggest ways to improve their partner's writing by using adjectives to describe feelings and places.

Whole class

Ask some children to read their accounts to the group. Ask the rest of the class to identify their favourite parts of the writing and make suggestions for improvement. Focus on whether the children have shown an awareness of their audience.

Lesson 4

Whole class

Tell the children that over the next two days they are going to write a book in the style of 'This is the Bear and the Scary Night' using their accounts of being lost or frightened. Explain to the children that they need to divide their story into sections and plan what is going to go on each page. Re-read the book with the children and, whilst reading, divide the story into sections noting down and numbering each section, *e.g.*

1. The bear is in the park. 2. The bear gets left behind. 3. The bear sees the moon. 4. The bear sees the eyes in the tree. 5. The owl takes the bear.

Group and independent work

Ask the children to divide and number their stories in a similar way.

Differentiation

Low Attainers – Allow this group to work with the teacher or an adult to sequence their oral accounts from the previous day into four simple sentences.

High Attainers – Encourage children to change their writing from first to third person, so that they are writing about a boy or a girl instead of themselves.

Whole class

Ask the children to evaluate the process of splitting their story up. What did they find difficult about this process? Ask the children to give examples using their work.

Lesson 5

Whole class

Recap on the pattern of the text with the children. Which lines of the text are repeated on each line of the book? Write up these lines to form a writing frame.
This is the _____
who _____
and _____
Write a short passage on the board using a narrative style, *e.g. 'One day I went to the shop with my mum. Suddenly I saw a toy which caught my eye and I went to have a look at it. When I turned around my mum had gone.'* Through shared writing, involve children in re-writing the passage in the style of the book, *e.g. This is the girl who went to the shop and wandered off.* Draw attention to the change from the first to third person when writing in the style of the text.

Group and independent work

Give each group several copies of Copymaster 4. Ask the children to use their plans from yesterday and write each page in the style of the text. This can be put together to make a book for each child.

Differentiation

Low Attainers – Give these children four copies of Copymaster 4. They can use their sentences from the previous lesson to write their books. Some adult support may be necessary.

High Attainers – Encourage children to work without the writing frame. Encourage them to vary the structure of some pages in a similar style to the book.

Whole class

Ask some children to read their stories to the class. Ask the rest of the class to comment on a part they liked and give any suggestions for improvement. (The children may need time outside the literacy hour to complete illustrations for their book.)

Objectives

Text level

- 3 To be aware of the difference between spoken and written language through comparing oral recounts with the text and to make use of formal story elements in re-telling;
- 4 To understand time and sequential relationships in stories, i.e. what happened when;
- 5 To identify and discuss reasons for events in stories, linked to plot;
- 6 To discuss familiar story themes and link to own experiences.

Sentence level

- 3 To recognise and take account of commas and exclamation marks in reading aloud with appropriate expression.

Word level

- 1 To secure identification, spelling and reading of long vowel digraphs in simple words from Year 1 Term 3 (ee/ea).

Resources

'Mog and the Vee Eee Tee' written by Judith Kerr (big book version if possible).
Copymaster 5, Copymaster 6. Homework 3.

Resource preparation

Enlarge Copymaster 5 and cut out each sentence. Photocopy Copymaster 6, cut into individual words and put each set of words into an envelope for the children to sort.
Make a 'story ladder' on a large piece of sugar paper (see Copymaster 5).

Assessment

At the end of this theme is the pupil able to:

- read and spell words containing the long vowel digraph ee/ea;
- understand time and sequential relationships in stories;
- recognise and take account of commas and exclamation marks and read aloud with appropriate expression?

Lesson 1

Whole class

Introduce the text to the children, locating the title, author and publisher. Look at the title of the book with the children. Can anyone identify what 'Vee Eee Tee' means? Ask the children to make simple predictions about the plot from the title. Do they think that the cat likes to go to the vet? Allow the children to recall some of their own accounts of taking their pets to the vet. Read the text with the children to the point where Mog is taken to the vet in the car.

Discuss with the children the use of expression in their reading. What tells a reader to pause or take a breath? Recap on the term 'comma' with the children and establish a simple definition. Re-read the text with the children and ask them to clap every time they see a comma. Encourage the children to take account of the commas when reading the text, i.e. take a breath. Ask the children to predict what will happen to Mog when

they get to the vet. Give pairs of children 'time out' to discuss this. Ask the children to feed back their ideas. Model how to record one of the ideas from the children designing a simple storyboard format.

Group and independent work

Ask the children to record their predictions about the end of the story using the storyboard format designed during the whole class session.

Differentiation

Low Attainers – Ask children to record their predictions pictorially, adding words and phrases with adult support if appropriate.
High Attainers – Ask children to focus on the correct use of punctuation in their writing.

Whole class

Ask some children to feed back their predictions. Without reading the text, look through the rest of the book and establish the end to the story. Compare the end of the story with the children's predictions.

Lesson 2

Whole class

Read the rest of the book with the children. Ask the children to re-tell the events in the story. Focus on the reasons for events in the story linked to the plot, *e.g.*
What was the reason for taking Mog to the vet?
How did he hurt his paw?
Look at the title of the story with the children and ask them to identify the spelling pattern in the words 'Vee Eee Tee'. Ask the children to brainstorm any other words which make the long 'ee' sound, asking the children if they know how to spell the words. Discuss how the long 'ee' sound can be made using the spelling pattern 'ea' or 'ee'. Record these words in three columns, 'ee', 'ea' and others. Put the children into pairs and give each pair a whiteboard. Give the children some

examples of words containing the long vowel digraph 'ee' (need, seat, week, speak, green, bean). Ask the children to record each word and then show their spelling to the rest of the class.

Group and independent work

Give pairs of children words from Copymaster 6 cut up and put into envelopes. Ask the children to sort the words on a large piece of paper into three columns, 'ee', 'ea' and others.

Differentiation

This activity can be completed in mixed ability pairs.

Whole class

Choose some children to write any words of their own into the correct column. Ask the children if they can identify any patterns for the words in each column.

Lesson 3

Whole class

Ask the children to re-tell the story orally around a circle, asking each child to add the next sentence. Compare the told story with the story in the text. Show the children the pieces of text which have been cut up from Copymaster 5. Read each piece of text with the children. Give the text to some children to hold at the front of the class. Ask the rest of the class to help the children to arrange themselves into the correct order, according to where the text comes in the story. Ask the children if they think that the text is complete. Show the children a blank story ladder that has been drawn onto a large piece of sugar paper (this should be in the same format as Copymaster 5 but without the text). Ask the children to stick pieces of text onto the ladder. Discuss where there needs to be gaps in the ladder to add missing pieces of the story. The final ladder should look the same as Copymaster 5. Using the shared writing

process, add a piece of text to the story ladder which could fill in the first gap, focusing on the sequence of events in the story.

Group and independent work

Give each child a copy of the story ladder on Copymaster 5. Ask the children to add sentences into the gaps in the ladder to sequence the story.

Differentiation

Low Attainers – Ask the children to sequence the story pictorially in four stages.
High Attainers – Encourage children to add more detail into the gaps in their ladder, using two or more sentences for each gap. You may wish to give this group an enlarged version of Copymaster 5.

Whole class

Using the story ladder from the whole class session, ask the children to look at their work and help you fill in the gaps on the ladder.

Lesson 4

Whole class

Explain to the children that in order to make their stories interesting, they should try to use words other than 'and' to begin and join sentences. Re-read the text with the children and ask them to put up their hands when they notice any words other than 'and' used to begin a sentence or join two ideas together. Make a class list. Write two short sentences on the board, *e.g. I was walking in the woods. I saw a man running.* Ask the children to use one of the words you have collected to join these sentences to make one sentence, *e.g. I was walking in the woods when I saw a man running.* Repeat this process with other sentences.

Group and independent work

Give each group a selection of texts. Ask pairs of children to look for examples of interesting words which begin or join sentences. Ask the children to use three of the words they have found in new sentences.

Differentiation

This activity gives the children the opportunity to work in mixed ability pairs.

Whole class

Ask the children to add new words they have discovered to the class list. Choose some children to read out the sentences they have written which contain joining words.

Lesson 5

Whole class

With the children re-read the beginning of the story up to the point where Mog arrives at the vet's. Tell the children that today they are going to think about the story from Mog's point of view. Ask the children to brainstorm some words which could describe Mog's feelings at different times in the story. List these. Ask the children to re-tell the story around a circle, but from Mog's point of view. Discuss the language used when telling a story in the first person. Pass an object around the circle (a toy cat is good for this) and ask the children to tell parts of the story from Mog's point of view. The teacher can interrupt to ensure the correct use of tense. Encourage the children to describe Mog's feelings at different times in the story. Through shared writing, begin to write the story from Mog's point of view. Focus on the correct use of tense and the description of Mog's feelings. You may wish to construct a frame or use the

story ladder from the previous lesson to help children to sequence the story.

Group and independent work

Ask the children to write the story from Mog's point of view, using the story ladder from the previous session to help sequence the story.

Differentiation

Low Attainers – Ask the children to re-tell the story from Mog's point of view. You may ask them to record their stories.
High Attainers – Encourage the children to think about the use of interesting words to join and begin sentences. Encourage them to use adjectives to describe Mog's feelings.

Whole class

Ask the children to re-tell the story from Mog's point of view. Focus on the description of Mog's feelings at each point of the story.

Objectives

Text level

- 6 To discuss familiar story themes and link to own experiences;
- 10 To use story structure to write about their own experience in same/similar form;
- 11 To use the language of time to structure a sequence of events.

Sentence level

- 4 To re-read own writing for sense and punctuation.

Resources

'Mog and the Vee Eee Tee' by Judith Kerr.

Copymaster 7, Copymaster 8. Homework 4.

Resource preparation

Photocopy an enlarged version of Copymaster 7 and Copymaster 8.

Assessment

At the end of this theme is the pupil able to:

- use a given story structure to write their own story in a similar style;
- use the language of time when structuring a sequence of events;
- re-read their own writing and check for sense and punctuation?

Lesson 1

Whole class

Remind the children of the story from the previous week. Ask the children whether they have any experience of taking pets to the vet. Ask the children what they think makes a good story. Would this story have been as good if Mog had liked the vet and was well behaved? Tell the children that most good stories have a problem which makes them interesting to read. Tell the children that this week they are going to write their own stories about taking a pet to the vet. Tell the children that they may wish to base the story around one of their own pets or an animal they know, or they may wish to create their own character. Look at a picture of Mog and ask children to think of some words which they could use to describe Mog. Encourage the children to describe his appearance and his personality. List their responses. Ask the children to think about the

animal that they are going to use in their story. Give children 'time out' to describe their chosen character to their partner. Ask some of the children to describe their partner's character to the rest of the class.

Group and independent work

Ask the children to choose a main character for their story. Ask them to draw and describe their character, thinking about appearance and personality.

Differentiation

Low Attainers – Ask children to draw a picture of their animal. They can add descriptive words with adult support.

High Attainers – Ask the children to include details such as favourite food, best trick.

Lesson 2

Whole class

Tell the children that they are going to write a plan for their stories. Show the children an enlarged copy of Copymaster 7. Use this to plan a story together. Use the 'time out' strategy to allow the children to discuss ideas. Focus discussion on the problem in the story. Ask the children to identify the problem when the family takes Mog to the vet. Ask the children to think about the problem that will occur in their own stories when their pet is taken to the vet's. Tell the children that most stories end with a solution to the problem. Can they identify the solution in 'Mog and the Vee Eee Tee'? Ask the children to think about the solution in their stories. How will their problem be solved?

Group and independent work

Give each child a copy of Copymaster 7. Ask the children to write a plan for their stories using the ideas they have discussed in the whole class session.

Differentiation

Low Attainers – Ask children to plan their stories in a sequence of three pictures, considering the beginning, middle and end.

High Attainers – Encourage children to include descriptions of settings and feelings of characters in their stories.

Whole class

Ask some of the children to present their story plans to the rest of the class. Encourage the use of questioning to clarify events and ideas.

Lesson 3
Whole class

Tell the children that they are going to write the first part of their version of 'Mog and the Vee Eee Tee'. Read the opening page with them. Focus on the opening line of the story. Can the children think of other ways to begin a story? Look at a selection of fiction texts and focus on the opening sentences of these stories. Make a list of the information that the children should include in the opening of their story, *e.g. introducing characters, describing the setting, setting the scene for the problem in the story.*
Using 'Mog and the Vee Eee Tee', make a list of events that the children will need to include in the opening section of their story. Remind them of ways to begin and join sentences in a story, using words other than 'and'. Discuss phrases relating to the passing of time, *e.g. first, meantime, at last, eventually.* Make a class list of these phrases for the children to include in their stories. Ask the children to think of the opening line to their story and tell the rest of the class.

Group and independent work
Ask the children to write the beginning of their stories, up to the point where their pet arrives at the vet's. Encourage the children to follow the structure which has been recorded in Lesson 2. If necessary remind the children that they are writing the story about the pet and not about themselves.

Differentiation
Low Attainers – Ask the children to add sentences to their picture sequences from the previous day.
High Attainers – Encourage children to use the correct punctuation in their work. Tell them to think carefully about their choice of adjectives when describing settings, characters and feelings.

Whole class
Ask some of the children to read their story openings to the class. Refer back to the list, which was made in the whole class session. Discuss whether sufficient detail has been included in the children's openings.

Lesson 4
Whole class

Tell the children that during this lesson they are going to add the problem to their story and write their endings. Read the middle section of 'Mog and the Vee Eee Tee' with the children. Ask them to identify ways in which the author has managed to create the feeling of chaos in their story. Ask a few children to take on the roles of the people in the vet's surgery. Ask those children to pretend to be the characters whilst the teacher narrates the story. Remind them of their story plans and ask them to identify the problem in their story. Use the 'time out' strategy to allow the children to discuss their ideas. Ask some children to feed back their ideas. Identify and discuss strengths and weaknesses. Tell the children that most stories come to an end when the problem is resolved. Ask them to identify the way in which the problem in their story will be resolved. Use the 'time out' strategy to allow them to discuss their ideas. Read the last two pages of 'Mog and the Vee Eee Tee' with the children. How does the author end the story? Why do they think the author uses a happy ending?

Group and independent work
Ask the children to complete their stories. Remind them to describe the problem and them resolve it at the end.

Differentiation
Low Attainers – Ask children to add an extra illustration to their work that will give their story a happy ending. They can then add text to their picture if appropriate.
High Attainers – Encourage children to add an extra twist to the end of their story in a similar style to 'Mog and the Vee Eee Tee'. Ask them to read each other's story endings and make suggestions for improvements.

Lesson 5
Whole class

Show the children an enlarged version of Copymaster 8. Tell them that this story is written in the style of 'Mog and the Vee Eee Tee' but the writer needs the children's help to check spellings and punctuation. Read through Copymaster 8 with the children and ask them to show you a sign when they think that the writing needs a full stop and a capital letter, *e.g. hand out for a full stop and hand on their heads for a capital letter.* Add the correct punctuation to Copymaster 8. Ask the children if they spotted any spelling mistakes in the piece of writing. Ask them to identify these and give the correct spellings for these words. Look at the use of 'and' on Copymaster 8. Ask them if they can think of any words to replace 'and' which will make the writing more interesting. Re-read the amended text on Copymaster 8 with the children.

Group and independent work
Ask pairs of children to read their work to each other. Can the children identify places where full stops may be needed? Ask the pairs to identify three spelling mistakes in each other's work and correct these.

Differentiation
Low Attainers – Children can work with an adult to check their spellings or focus on the spelling of simple high frequency words using the 'look, say, cover, write and check' method.
High Attainers – Encourage these children to identify where their partner has used 'and' and to suggest words to replace it. Ask the children to check their partner's use of commas, speech marks and exclamation marks.

Whole class
Ask children to read their story to another partner. Ask them what they liked about their partner's story. Discuss what makes a good story.

Objectives

Text level

- 3 To be aware of the difference between spoken and written language through comparing oral recounts with text and to make use of formal story elements in retelling;
- 4 To understand time and sequential relationships in stories, i.e. what happened when.

Sentence level

- 6 To use boxes and arrows as simple organisational devices to indicate sequence.

Word level

- 7 To use word ending 'ed' (past tense) to support reading and spelling.

Resources

'Mr. Gumpy's Outing' by John Burningham
'Mr. Gumpy's Motor Car' by John Burningham

A selection of simple stories with familiar settings which take place over a day or a short period of time and can be detected through the illustrations, e.g. 'Peace at Last' by Jill Murphy, 'When the moon looked in at the window' by Sheila McCullagh, 'Billy and Belle' by Sarah Garland, 'Once upon a time' by John Prater, 'We're going on a bear hunt' by Michael Rosen and Helen Oxenbury. Copymaster 9, Copymaster 10, Copymaster 11. Homework 5.

Assessment

At the end of this theme is the pupil able to:

- show an awareness of the difference between recounts and the language of the text;
- understand how simple stories are sequences and make simple plans to show story sequence;
- show an awareness of past tense 'ed' endings?

Lesson 1

Whole class

Introduce 'Mr. Gumpy's Outing' to the children. Explain that over the next two weeks they are going to write another story about Mr. Gumpy.
Show the children the first page of the story. Ask the children to read the sentence. Ask the children to look at the illustration and decide what time of day it could be, *e.g. morning, afternoon or night-time*. On an enlarged copy of Copymaster 9 note the answer. Ask the children to give reasons for their choices. Turn to the final page of the story. Read the text together. Look at the illustration and again ask the children what time of day it might be. Ask the children to give reasons for their choices. Note when the story ends on Copymaster 9.

Group and independent work

Give children a selection of simple stories with familiar settings that take place over a short period of time, *e.g. one day, one night*. Using Copymaster 9, ask children to note the title of the book and then decide what time of day the story begins and when the story ends by looking at the illustrations at the beginning and end of the book.

Differentiation

Low Attainers – Carry out the activity orally. An adult could write on to the grid.
High Attainers – Ask children to write reasons for their decisions.

Whole class

Choose a selection of texts the children have been using. Ask the children to use their completed grids to say when the stories begin and end.

Lesson 2

Whole class

Read 'Mr. Gumpy's Outing' with the whole class. Discuss how the story takes place over one day and relate to Lesson 1.
Give the children 'time out' to discuss with a partner at least three events that happened in the story during the course of the day.

e.g.   Mr. Gumpy went out in his boat.
         All the animals wanted to go with him.
         The animals did not stay still in the boat.
         Everyone fell into the water.
         They climbed out of the water.
         They walked to Mr. Gumpy's house for tea.

Ask pairs to feed back. Write the first two main events onto separate pieces of paper and stick them onto a board in front of the class. Talk through the whole of the story but do not write all the events onto paper.

Group and independent work

Give pairs of children six squares of paper. Ask them to copy the first two events from the board and write the next four events together. Tell them that they must tell the whole of the story in these six sentences. Tell them to stick their squares of paper onto a paper strip in the correct order and draw an arrow between each event to show progression through the story.

Differentiation

Low Attainers – Let children look through the book again and ask them to talk about the story. Copy the first two events from the board and then draw four pictures to show what happened in the rest of the story.
High Attainers – Encourage children to write short and specific sentences.

Whole class

Children bring their work and sit with their partner. Sequence the rest of the story, writing four more events onto paper, taking ideas from the children. Stick the six individual pieces of paper in a line on the board. Draw an arrow between each event to show progression. Save this storyboard for future lessons.

Lesson 3

Whole class

Give the children parts to read from the story, i.e. Mr. Gumpy, the children, the rabbit, the cat, the dog, the pig, the sheep, the chickens, the calf and the goat. Read the text, with you as narrator. Refer back to the sequence of events from Lesson 2. Ask the children how the reading of the story today is different from the sequencing of events yesterday. Highlight differences, such as lack of detail, dialogue and characterisation start. Discuss the difference between what the text says and how you tell someone what the story is about.

Group and independent work

Groups of children act out the story. (Cut down the number of animals.) Encourage children to use language from the text. Tell the children to try to remember the sequence of the story so that the events are in the correct order.

Differentiation

High Attainers – Act out the story with one child as narrator.

Whole class

Groups perform their plays to the rest of the class. Tell the audience to listen for language from the text and whether the story is in the correct sequence.

Lesson 4

Whole class

Write on the board 'Mr. Gumpy told the children not to squabble.' Ask the children to read the sentence and then think what Mr. Gumpy said to the other characters. Either, write similar sentences and make a list or use prepared sentence strips (from Copymaster 10) and order them with the children. Read the sentences together.
Write on the board:
'For a little while they all went along happily but then …
The goat …
The calf …'
Continue to the end of the page omitting the verbs. Discuss the words that should be added to complete the text. List the missing verbs. Read the text together. Ask the children to look for the pattern, drawing attention to the 'ed' ending.

Group and independent work

Using Copymaster 10 as a prompt, ask the children to complete their own page starting 'For a little while they all went along happily but then …' They can write the names of the animals and stick the appropriate verbs in place.

Differentiation

Low Attainers – Use sentence strips to sequence the animals' actions and use the text to help with the order.
High Attainers – Write the page from memory without help from Copymaster 10.

Whole class

Write up the following words:

help	helped
rush	rushed
chase	chased
trample	trampled

Ask the children to read the words and look for the pattern. Ask the children if they can remember any rules for adding an 'ed' suffix to a word. Give pairs of children a word from the list and ask them to put it into a sentence. Ask the pairs to tell the rest of the class their sentence.

Lesson 5

Whole class

Show the children 'Mr. Gumpy's Motor Car' and read the story together. Give the childen 'time out' to discuss the main events in the story. Write the events on pieces of paper, as in Lesson 2. Use the same number of events. Stick the sequence of events below the sequence from the first story. Draw arrows between each event to show the sequence. Read both story sequences with the children. Use Copymaster 11 to find similarities and differences. Do this orally.

Group and independent word

In pairs, ask the children to think about the two stories and to complete Copymaster 11. Some children may need to refer to the texts.

Differentiation

Low Attainers – Carry out the activity orally, making reference to the two books.
High Attainers – Work with a partner unaided.

Whole class

Discuss the similarities and differences with the whole class.

Theme 6 — Stories with familiar settings – Mr. Gumpy's Outing (week 2)

Objectives

Text level
• 10 To use a story structure to write another story in a similar form. (Note: children may relate the story to their own experience, but will not write about their own experience.)

Sentence level
• 4 To re-read own writing for sense and punctuation.

Resources
'Mr. Gumpy's Outing' by John Burningham
Class story sequence from week 1.
Copymaster 12. Homework 6.

Assessment
At the end of this theme is the pupil able to:
• write a simple story based on a story sequence plan, making reference to the text model?

Lesson 1

Whole class

Remind the children of last week's literacy work. Ask them to recall the sequence of 'Mr. Gumpy's Outing'. (You may wish to ask children about their homework and the sequences they found in their chosen books.) Run through the sequence orally and check it against the written sequence from last week. Remind the children of the second text, 'Mr. Gumpy's Motor Car'. Tell them that this week they are going to write their own story about Mr. Gumpy. Have blank paper displayed below the story sequences from last week. Look at the first box of the story sequence. Ask the children to discuss in pairs what else Mr. Gumpy could do. Collect ideas and write in the empty box, *e.g. Mr. Gumpy could go out in his plane, go to the seaside, go to the shops.* Look at the second box and ask the children who might want to go with him. Choose two or three characters only. Children may want to include some of the same characters. Pick one scenario and work it through to the end of the sequence. Pay particular attention to the problems that could happen, *e.g. In Mr. Gumpy's Outing the animals did not stay still in the boat and they all fell into the water.* Write in note form giving minimal detail.

Group and independent work
Children plan their story using Copymaster 12. Tell the children to refer to the whole class plan if they need to. Reinforce the idea that this is only a plan. They do not need to write their story, as they will start that tomorrow.

Differentiation
Low Attainers – Work on a group plan with adult help.

Whole class
Ask some children to read their sequences to the rest of the class. Draw attention to the 'problems' in the sequences.

Lesson 2

Whole class

Use the whole class plan produced in Lesson 1 to model the writing of the beginning of the story. Use an enlarged format of the type of book you will give the children for their stories, *e.g. zig-zag, stapled sheets.* Ensure that the book has 6 pages (plus front and back cover) so that the children can link each page to one incident in their story sequence. Model writing the first two pages of the story, talking aloud as you write. Use similar language to the text in 'Mr. Gumpy's Outing'. Ask the children to read what you have written. Would they like to make any changes? Ask the children to look at the punctuation and spelling. (You could make deliberate mistakes, *e.g. miss out capital letters in Mr. Gumpy's name.*)
Discuss how you might illustrate the first two events. Quickly sketch these into the class book. Compare the sequence plan and the story so far.

Group and independent work
Ask the children to write the first two pages of their book using the sequence plan to help them. When they are happy with the text they can add illustrations.

Differentiation
Low Attainers – Children work on their group plan and compose the beginning of the story. Support the writing of the first page by individual children. Encourage children to read their first page to the group when they have finished.
High Attainers – Encourage children to think carefully about their choice of phrases. They may wish to refer to 'Mr. Gumpy's Outing' or 'Mr. Gumpy's Motor Car'.

Whole class
Give all children a piece of paper and pencil. (Children could remain in their places for this activity). Ask the children to think of words they have used today that they are not sure how to spell. Help children to work them out for themselves using phonic knowledge if appropriate. If not, guide the children in spelling the word correctly, encouraging them to 'have a go' themselves first. Show the children the correct spelling. Tell the children to write the correct spelling beside their attempt.

Lesson 3

Whole class

Involve the children in the shared writing of the next two pages of the class book. Continue to use the class sequence plan from Lesson 1. Discuss the problem and what happens to the characters. Give children 'time out' in pairs to think about what the characters might say. Encourage the children to re-read as you are writing. Involve individuals in the writing process. Give the children their work from yesterday and their story sequence sheet. Tell them to read what they have done so far to a partner and then ask them to explain to their partner what will happen next. Support low attaining children in discussion.

Group and independent work

Ask children to continue writing and illustrating the next two pages of their story.

Differentiation

Low Attainers – Support as in Lesson 2, or ask children to continue illustrating their stories independently.
High Attainers – Tell the children to re-read their work as they write and to make any necessary corrections.

Whole class

Ask the children who have been working with adult support to read their stories so far. Model a comment on the way the work has been written, *e.g. 'I like ... because ...'* Ask other children to comment on the work in a similar way.

Lesson 4

Whole class

Return to the class sequence plan and tell the children that you are going to think about the last two pages of the story. Give children 'time out' in pairs to think about how the next page might begin. Write some examples on the board. Read them together and decide which one would be best. Don't write more, but move onto the last page. Look at the last page of 'Mr. Gumpy's Outing' and read together. Compare with the last page of 'Mr. Gumpy's Motor Car'. Ask the children what is different.

Compose the last page of the class story using the same format.

Group and independent work

Children complete their stories.

Differentiation

Low Attainers – Support children in composing orally and scribe for individually where appropriate.

Whole class

Ask the children who have been working with adult support to read the end of their stories.

Lesson 5

Whole class

Write up examples of various children's work in order to draw attention to:
• style of writing and good use of vocabulary;
• spelling and sentence punctuation.
Read together, discuss and correct.
Give children their work. Tell them that they need to think of a title for their story. Ask children to read their work to themselves and think about their title. Support low attainers. Write up a couple of examples of titles.

Group and independent work

Children add a title and complete the front cover of their book. Ask them to practise reading their story when they have finished.

Differentiation

High Attainers – Work with the group, encouraging the children to read, discuss and make suggestions for improving their work.

Whole class

Children sit in a circle and evaluate the two weeks, work. Go around the circle and ask children to say what they liked about the work. Go around the circle and ask them to say if there were things they found difficult. Ask the children what they would like to do with their finished books, *e.g. display, read to younger children, put in the book corner.*

Theme 7) Poems with familiar settings (week 1)

Objectives

Text level

- 7 To learn, re-read and recite favourite poems, taking account of punctuation and to comment on aspects such as word combinations, sound patterns (such as rhymes, rhythms, alliterative patterns) and forms of presentation;
- 8 To collect and categorise poems to build class anthologies;
- 12 To use simple poetry structures and to substitute own ideas, write new lines.

Sentence level

- 3 To recognise and take account of commas and exclamation marks in reading aloud with appropriate expression;
- 3 To revise knowledge about uses of capitalisation for titles and emphasis.

Word level

- 10 To build individual collections of significant words.

Resources

'Night-time, Fright-time' (Copymaster 13) from 'You Little Monkey and other poems for young children' by John Foster.
'After Dark' (Copymaster 15) from 'Tea in the Sugar Bowl, Potato in my Shoe' by Michael Rosen.
Copymaster 14.
A collection of anthologies containing poems related to night-time, feelings associated with going to bed.
Homework 7.

Assessment

At the end of this theme is the pupil able to:
- read and recite with expression all or parts of a favourite poem associated with the focus;
- read and categotise poems;
- substitute own ideas and write new lines for familiar poems?

Lesson 1

Whole class

Read 'Night-time, Fright-time' by John Foster (Copymaster 13) to the children without showing them the text.
Ask the class if they have ever felt like the person in this poem.
Write up some two-word phrases from the poem, *e.g. Shadows creep; Floorboards creak; Ghost glides; Darkness hides.* Ask the children to describe the picture these phrases bring to mind.
Show the children the text and read it together with the appropriate expression. Draw attention to the capitalisation in the last line. Practise ways of reading this line.
Read the poem together again and ask the children whether they can recognise a pattern in its organisation,i.e. 1st, 3rd, 5th and 7th verses are the same, every verse starts with 'Night-time'.
Split the class into two groups. Read the poem aloud with one group reading verses 1, 3, 5 and 7 and the other group reading verses 2, 4 and 6.

Group and independent work

- Using Copymaster 14, ask children to cut up the words and reassemble them into the most powerful phrases. Encourage them to read the words in a variety of combinations before they make up their minds.
- Children search a collection of poetry anthologies for poems which create a similar effect to 'Night-time, Fright-time'. Keep these for use later in the week.

Differentiation

Low Attainers – Cut the poem on Copymaster 13 into individual verses. Ask the children, in pairs, to sequence the poem and learn the repeated verse.
High Attainers – Give individual children whiteboards and pens. Ask the children to think of their own two-word phrases. Tell the children to try out different combinations and prepare four phrases to read to the class.

Whole class

Using first words from Copymaster 14, ask children to supply the most appropriate second word of the phrase. Discuss choices. Collect some two-word phrases from group working on whiteboards and add to the class list.

Lesson 2

Whole class

Ask the children if they can remember the repeated two lines of the poem read in Lesson 1. Check with the poem. Read the poem again together with expression. Look at the structure of verses 2, 4 and 6. Highlight rhyme – creep, sleep – hides, glides. Make use of the 'time out' strategy and ask pairs of children to think of words that rhyme with 'creep' (peep, sheep, weep) and 'hides' (slides, rides).
Cover verse two and re-write using children's phrases generated in Lesson 1. Ask the children to read the new verse to their partner.

Group and individual work

Rewrite verses four and six individually using prepared phrases from Lesson 1.

Differentiation

Low Attainers – Use a selection of prepared phrases from Lesson 1 to write another verse.
High Attainers – Think about the sounds of words and the rhyme at the end of the line. Read each verse with a partner.

Whole class

Choose children to recite verse 1 and read or recite one of the verses they have written.

Lesson 3

Whole class

Read 'After Dark' by Michael Rosen (Copymaster 15).
Look at the pattern of the poem and the use of the
phrase 'After dark'.
Discuss the effect of this poem and compare with 'Night-
time, Fright-time'.
Ask the children how this poem is different from 'Night-
time, Fright-time', *e.g. it does not rhyme.* Draw attention
to the structure of the poem and where the poet has
started a new line. As a whole class, read the poem.

Group and independent work

• Copy the poem and cut it into individual lines. Children
work with a partner, read the lines and reassemble
into the poem.
• Search a collection of poetry anthologies for poems on
a similar theme.
• Children who found a poem earlier in the week copy it
for inclusion in a class anthology.

Lesson 4

Whole class

Read the first verse of 'After Dark' to the children.
Write up 'Outside after dark'. Give children 'time out' in
pairs to think of an alternative second line. Discuss
children's ideas. Write two examples with the children
and conclude the verse 'after dark, after dark.' Read the
verse with the class. Is it as good as a verse in the
published poem? Ask children to justify their opinions.
Read the published verse and class written verses
together.
Discuss possible new titles for this poem, *e.g. Outside After
Dark.* Discuss the use of capitalisation for each word in
the title. Give children opportunities to investigate
capitalisation in other titles.

Group and independent work

Children write individual poems based on the verse
beginning 'In here after dark'.

Differentiation

Low Attainers – Give children the first and third line of the
poem. Ask them to think of the second line and write it
in. Children can read their new verses to a partner.

Whole class

Sit in a circle. Go around the circle and ask children to
read their poems or new verses.

Lesson 5

Whole class

Enlarge and read together examples of children's work
from Lesson 4. Pick out features to praise. Discuss:
• choice of words;
• layout of the verse; (Have the children remembered to
start a new line in the appropriate place?)
• use of punctuation, particularly the use of the comma
in the last line.

Group and independent work

Ask the children to read through their own work and
make any changes that are necessary following class
discussion. Tell the children to choose the best verse
they have written and copy it out. Groups mount their
finished work as one poem ready for inclusion in the
class anthology and give the poem a title.

Whole class

Children sit in a circle. Evaluate the work with the class.
Children can offer a comment about the work in turn,
*e.g. what they liked or did not like; if they were pleased with
their work and why; which poem they liked best and why.*
This can inform evaluation of the work.

Theme 8) Poems with familiar settings (week 2)

Objectives

Text level
- 8 To collect and categorise poems to build class anthologies;
- 9 Through shared and guided writing to apply phonological, graphic knowledge and sight vocabulary to spell words accurately;
- 12 To use simple poetry structures and substitute own ideas.

Sentence level
- 4 To re-read own writing for sense and punctuation.

- 5 To revise use of capitalisation for emphasis.

Resources
Homework 8.

Assessment
At the end of this theme is the pupil able to:
- write simple poems based on a shared class composition;
- re-read own writing and make simple changes to content and punctuation where necessary?

Lesson 1
Whole class

Discuss with the children the poems read last week. Show the children the on-going preparation of the class anthology containing:
- children's writing based on the focus poems from week 1
- poems on a similar theme, copied from a range of poetry books and anthologies.

Tell the children that the focus of this week is to write their own poems about 'In Bed At Night'.
Return to 'After Dark' by Michael Rosen and read verse 3. Remind the children of the poems and phrases they composed. If necessary re-read some of these.
Write on the board:
- What can you hear?
- What can you see?
- How do you feel?

Read these questions with the children. Ask them to close their eyes and imagine they are in bed at night and think about what they might hear, see and feel.
Give children 'time out' to discuss this with a partner.
Write on a large piece of paper 'In bed at night I hear ...'

Ask the children for their ideas and add to the line. Start each idea with 'In bed at night I hear ...'. Re-read each line as you write. Discuss the choice of vocabulary. Re-read the poem when you have generated four lines.

Group and independent work
- Ask children to write their own four line 'In bed at night I hear ...' poem. Tell them they can use one line from the class poem as a start if they wish.
- Continue finding, reading and writing out poems with a night-time theme for the class anthology.

Differentiation
Low Attainers – Use whiteboards with 'In bed at night I hear' written on them. Children add to the line and write one more line individually.
High Attainers – Think about their word choices and the pictures they are creating for the reader.
Photocopy work from the whiteboards at the end of the lesson.

Whole class
Children sit in a circle and share their favourite line from their poem. Ask the class if there were any lines they particularly liked and why. Write them up.

Lesson 2
Whole class

Ask children to sit in a circle. Give children their work from Lesson 1. Ask children to read their poems to a partner and then read their partner's poem. Ask children to comment on what they liked about each other's work. Focus attention on good use of vocabulary.
Tell the children that they are going to think about and write the next verse of their poem.
Write up 'In bed at night I see'. Give children 'time out' to discuss this with a partner. Ask children for suggestions to complete the line. Discuss the effect of some of their suggestions.

Group and independent work
Children write the next four line verse of their poem individually. Remind the children to start each line 'In bed at night I see'.

Differentiation
Low Attainers – An adult writes for the group. Prepare a group reading of the poem when finished.
High Attainers – Before starting, read 'In bed at night I hear' from Lesson 1 to yourself and make this poem lead on from it.

Whole class
Children read their group poem. Encourage others to comment on the images it creates and use of vocabulary.

Lesson 3
Whole class

Explain to children that they are going to write the third verse of their poem.
Write up 'In bed at night I feel'. Give pairs of children a whiteboard and pen. Tell the children to work with their partner and think of how they might feel, discuss together and write the end of the line onto their whiteboard. Support the low attainers. Read examples and discuss choices of words. Give children time in their pairs to think of another line or improve the first one they have written. Read again with the whole class.

Group and independent work
In the same pairs write the third verse of the poem with each line beginning 'In bed at night I feel'. Use the ideas generated in whole class work as the first line.

Differentiation
Low Attainers – Continue writing 'In bed at night I feel' on whiteboards with adult help if appropriate.
High Attainers – Children read their first two verses ('In bed at night I hear' and 'In bed at night I see') to an adult and discuss choices of vocabulary and use of punctuation and spelling before starting the third verse.

Whole class
Collect examples of children's work. Tell the children to listen carefully to some lines from the poems. Choose individual children to comment on the line they liked best and try to explain why.

Lesson 4
Whole class

Enlarge or copy some examples of children's work from Lesson 3. Discuss the use of capitalisation for emphasis and choose words, phrases or a line to write in capital letters. Encourage children to read with appropriate expression. Discuss how the use of emphasis adds to the poem. Give pairs of children 'time out' to find a phrase that creates a 'scary' effect. Ask them why. Pick a phrase that could be improved by changing the adjective. Ask the children to think of alternative words. Choose one and substitute the chosen phrase. Re-read the poems with changes.

Group and independent work
Children read their own work and make improvements and changes according to teacher's comments and discussion from the whole class session.

Differentiation
Low Attainers – Copy out verse from Lesson 1 and group verse from Lesson 2 for the class anthology.
High Attainers – Encourage children to re-read their work and decide how they might improve word choices, use of emphasis, spelling and use of punctuation.

Whole class
Write up words and phrases in various styles e.g. *very big, very small, rounded, bold, with full stops in between the words.* Give individual children or pairs whiteboards and phrases to write in different styles. Practise reading in different ways and discuss how different effects can change the reading and emphasis of the poem.

Lesson 5
Whole class

Rehearse and group read verses written by children onto tape. Listen to taped version and discuss expression used in the reading.

Group and independent work
Copy out poems and illustrate for class anthology.

Whole class
Give individual children or pairs whiteboards and ask them to evaluate the week's work and write a brief comment about it. Share with the class. Write a class evaluation which could be displayed with finished work, e.g. *we liked writing our poems because …*

This is a two week unit of work which moves the children from reading and discussing the key features of a range of instructions to writing their own set of instructions.

Objectives

Text level

- 13 To read simple written instructions in the classroom, simple recipes, plans, instructions for constructing something;
- 14 To note key structural features;
- 15 To write simple instructions;
- 16 To use models from reading to organise instructions sequentially;
- 17 To use diagrams in instructions;
- 18 To use appropriate register in written instructions.

Sentence level

- 3 To find examples in fiction and non-fiction of words and phrases that link sentences;
- 6 To use a variety of simple organisational devices to indicate sequences and relationships.

Resources

A display of a selection of instructions from a range of sources, *e.g. recipes, D.I.Y. plans, construction instructions, instructions for making gifts or decorations.*
A children's recipe book and art and craft book.
A set of instructions for making a simple card, gift or hat. (This fits in well around Christmas time.)
Copymaster 16. Homework 9.

Resource preparation

Find 3 or 4 simple recipes or sets of instructions to use in shared reading time. (Children's recipe or art and craft books are a good resource for this.) Select a recipe to cut up into sections ready for re-organisation.
Cut Copymaster 16 into sections, enough for one between two.

Assessment

At the end of this theme is the pupil able to:
- explain the key features of instructions;
- write simple instructions which use some of these key features;
- use words or phrases which link sentences, appropriate to the form of instructions?

Lesson 1

Whole class

Introduce the unit by giving a child a simple instruction to follow, *e.g. walk over to the table, pull out a chair and sit down.* Discuss what you have just asked that child to do. During the discussion draw out the word instruction. Ask the children to think of when and where they may have read and written instructions. Make use of the 'time out' strategy to discuss this in pairs. Make a class list. Model how to write a set of instructions based on the verbal instructions you gave the child at the beginning of the lesson. Draw children's attention to the series of steps in the instructions.

Group and independent work

Organise the children into pairs and ask them to think of a simple instruction to give their partner with no more than three or four steps. Tell the children to write their steps out in sentences and then to see if their partner can follow the instructions.
If a Roamer is available, one group can program a set of instructions for the Roamer to move to a given point in the room. This activity can then continue throughout the week with groups taking turns.

Differentiation

Low Attainers – Prepare a set of instructions verbally (this could be onto a tape recorder), or written with adult support.
High Attainers – Encourage the correct use of punctuation in the children's sentences.

Whole class

Some children can read their instructions to another child or the teacher to see if they can be followed accurately.

Lesson 2

Whole class

Draw the children's attention to the class display of instructions. Explain that you are going to be looking at lots of different instructions to find out how they are organised.
Introduce the children to a simple recipe. Ask the children to identify the type of text. Draw out the key organisational features of a set of instructions, including title headings, any use of numbers, pictures, diagrams, handy hints, safety tips etc.

Highlight these features and make a class list of them for future reference.

Group and independent work

Provide the children with a range of different instructions taken from a variety of sources. Ask the children to identify and highlight key organisational features.

Differentiation

Low Attainers – Highlight key features only, with adult support if necessary.
High Attainers – Ask the children to label key organisational features.

Lesson 3

Whole class

Revisit the list of key organisational features of instructions made in the previous lesson. Stick up the pieces of a set of instructions which have been cut into sections, i.e. title, steps of instruction, diagrams or illustrations. Ask the children to help you to place pieces of instructions in the correct location. Ask how they know where each piece should go. Draw attention to the title, any use of numbers and where pictures or diagrams should go. When complete, ask the children if there is anything they would add to the instructions, such as safety tips or extra diagrams.

Group and independent work

Using Copymaster 16 cut into sections, ask the children in pairs to stick the instructions onto a large sheet of paper in the correct order and add any other features.

Differentiation

This activity can be completed in mixed ability pairs.

Whole class

Ask children to explain the order of the instructions for making a fruit cocktail. Which words help to order them correctly?

Lesson 4

Whole class

Tell the children that you are going to look at the types of words which begin sentences in a set of instructions. Re-visit the set of instructions used in Lesson 2. Highlight sequential words, *e.g. next, finally,* in one colour and words which give a command (imperative), *e.g. mix or cut, in another colour.* Discuss and make a class list of words. Revisit the set of instructions written in Lesson 1 and ask the children to help you to select more appropriate words to begin each sentence and extend any sentences if appropriate.

Group and independent work

Children can write another set of instructions for performing a simple task with no more than three or four steps. You may wish to link this with another curricular area, *e.g. D and T, Science.* Focus on the use or sequential words and phrases encouraging the use of the class list for ideas.

Differentiation

Low Attainers – Give the children a set of simple instructions with the first word missing from each sentence. Ask them to select an appropriate word to begin each sentence.
High Attainers – Encourage the use of a variety of verbs and sequential words.

Whole class

Some children can read the first words from each sentence in their instructions. Can any new words be added to the class list?

Lesson 5

Whole class

Tell the children that they are going to follow a set of instructions. Show them the instructions, *e.g. making a card or hat.* Read the instructions, drawing attention to the use of key organisational features and language use.

Group and independent work

Children work in pairs and follow the instructions to make the finished product.

Differentiation

Low Attainers – Work in a small group with an adult reading the instructions.
High Attainers – Can the children think of ways of improving the instructions they have been given?

Whole class

Evaluate the set of instructions. What were the good and bad points? Make a list. How could we improve the instructions?

Theme 10 Instructions (week 2)

Objectives

Text level
- 13 To read simple written instructions in the classroom, simple recipes, plans, instructions for constructing something;
- 14 To note key structural features;
- 15 To write simple instructions;
- 16 To use models from reading to organise instructions sequentially;
- 17 To use diagrams in instructions;
- 18 To use appropriate register in written instructions.

Sentence level
- 2 To find examples in fiction and non-fiction, of words and phrases that link sentences;

- 6 To use a variety of simple organisational devices to indicate sequences and relationships.

Resources
1 sheet of newspaper for each child in the class. Copymaster 17. Homework 10.

Assessment
At the end of this theme is the pupil able to:
- explain the key features of instructions;
- write simple instructions which use some of these key features;
- use words or phrases which link sentences, appropriate to the form of instructions?

Lesson 1
Whole class

Recap on the term 'instructions' and draw the children's attention to the class display of various types of instructions. Revisit the list of key structural features of instructions made by the class during week 1. Give each child a sheet of newspaper and tell them that they need to follow the instructions you are going to give them to make a piece of clothing. Give a set of verbal instructions to make a simple triangular paper hat (Copymaster 17). When each child has made a paper hat, begin a shared writing activity asking the children to help you write a set of instructions for making the hat. Complete the title and the first two or three steps of the instructions as a whole class, with the teacher writing. Focus on layout and how to begin sentences as discussed during the previous week's work.

Group and independent work
Ask the children to copy and then complete the instructions for making a paper hat that are clear enough for someone else to follow. Provide the children with a sheet of paper large enough to have diagrams added during Lesson 2.

Differentiation
Low Attainers – In a series of boxes, draw the key steps for making the hat, adding words to go with each step where appropriate.
High Attainers – Children can make sure that they use a variety of verbs and sequential words. When they have completed their instructions, swap with a partner who checks for clarity and makes suggestions for improvement.

Whole class
Choose children to read out their instructions whilst the teacher follows them and makes a paper hat. Discuss the clarity of the instructions and ask other children to offer suggestions for improvement.

Lesson 2
Whole class

Show the children the set of instructions you began writing together during the previous lesson. Ask the children to think about the instructions they have looked at so far and suggest ways in which the instructions written yesterday could be improved in order to make them easier to follow.

Ask children to think about how, if someone could not read or spoke a different language, they would follow the instructions. Add any appropriate suggestions to the set of instructions, drawing particular attention to the use of diagrams.

Ask the children to suggest where the diagrams should go and whether they will need numbers, arrows or labels. Add diagrams to the first two steps of instructions.

Group and independent work
Give the children the instructions they completed in the previous lesson and ask them to add any key features which have been discussed, particularly the use of diagrams.

Differentiation
Low Attainers – Work with an adult to add a sentence to each of their diagrams completed during the previous lesson.
High Attainers – Can they use at least three different organisational features in their work?

Whole class
Ask the children to show a particular diagram to the class. Can they guess which step of the instruction it is illustrating? How do the diagrams help to make the instructions easier to follow?

Lesson 3

Whole class

Tell the children that over the next three days they are going to produce their own set of instructions for playing their favourite playground game. Use the 'time out' strategy for children to discuss their favourite game in pairs. Listen to discussion and highlight a game that is not too complicated. Ask one child to describe their favourite game to the rest of the class. Discuss the use of a brainstorm as the first stage in writing the instructions. Model this process using the game previously described. Record the name of the game in the centre of a large piece of paper and randomly record any rules, strategies or ideas for the game in sentences around the outside.

Group and independent work

Children complete their own brainstorm based around their favourite game. Encourage the children to choose a simple game, *e.g. 'It' or 'Tag'.*

Differentiation

Low Attainers – Complete a brainstorm as a group with adult support.
High Attainers – Consider key features of instructions when brainstorming.

Whole class

In pairs, children explain the initial stages of their game to a friend. Each child has to explain the start of their partner's game to the class.

Lesson 4

Whole class

Look at instructions for playing games from the class display. Discuss any features which have not been considered in the class instructions, *e.g. number of players or rules.*
Using these ideas, produce a class writing frame with key headings for the children to follow when writing their own set of instructions, *e.g. title, number of players, rules etc.*

Group and independent work

Children can use the set of headings produced in whole class work as a framework for writing instructions for their playground game in draft form.

Differentiation

Low Attainers – Complete instructions using diagrams and a grid format. A group set of written instructions can then be written with adult support.
High Attainers – Encourage children to add their own features to the writing frame and check spelling with a partner when the work is complete.

Whole class

Ask some children to read various sections of their instructions using the headings from the class frame. Draw attention to the appropriate use of instructional language.

Lesson 5

Whole class

Ask a child if they would mind having their work used as an example to see how it could be improved. Use this particular piece as a shared text. Read through and highlight all the positive features. Select one or two sentences for editing and ask the children to suggest ways in which the writing could be improved by substituting words or extending sentences. (This can be prepared beforehand.)
Discuss any ways in which diagrams, boxes, arrows and numbers could be used to make the instructions easier to follow.
Give the children their work and, using the 'time out' strategy, ask them to look at their friend's instructions and suggest two ways in which they could be improved.

Group and independent work

Use first drafts of instructions to complete a final draft, considering changes to text and the use of organisational devices to improve the quality of their work.

Differentiation

Low Attainers – Add diagrams to their set of group instructions or add a sentence to their own diagrams.
High Attainers – Children can edit their own spelling mistakes and improve at least one sentence before completing their final draft.

Whole class

Discuss with the children what they have learned about instructions over the past two weeks. Suggestions can be made into a class list and used to support assessment.

Theme 1 Traditional stories (character focus)

Objectives

Text level
- 6 To identify and describe characters;
- 14 To write simple descriptions of characters.

Sentence level
- 4 To be aware of the need for grammatical agreement in speech and writing, matching verbs to nouns/pronouns correctly;
- 8 To use commas to separate items in a list.

Word level
- 10 To build collections of significant words.

Resources
A collection of props/artefacts that can be used to identify and describe characters from traditional stories, e.g. *Little Red Riding Hood – red cape, basket, play food; Jack from Jack and the Beanstalk – packet of bean seeds, golden egg, picture of a giant.*

Word cards of items relating to characters.
A collection of traditional stories.
Copymasters 18 and 19. Homework 11.

Resource preparation
Collect resources and make into character 'bags' or 'boxes' for current and future use.

Assessment
At the end of this theme is the pupil able to:
- describe orally and write simple descriptions of characters;
- take on the role of a character;
- use commas to separate items in a list?

Lesson 1

Whole class

Show the children artefacts relating to a character from a traditional story. Ask the children if they can identify the character. Give pairs of children 'time out' to discuss the physical appearance of the character with a partner. Write the physical characteristics of the character on a board, taking suggestions from the children. Separate points with commas. Discuss the use of commas when writing a list.

Group and independent work
Give each group of children a collection of artefacts relating to a character. Ask the children to discuss who the character might be and which traditional story they come from. Ask the children to use the first part of Copymaster 18 to list artefacts and physical characteristics of their character. Remind them to make use of commas to separate the listed items.

Differentiation
Low Attainers – Match word cards with objects before making a list.
High Attainers – Encourage the use of a thesaurus to develop descriptive vocabulary.

Whole class
Group members read out their lists of physical characteristics. The class have to guess who they are describing.

Lesson 2

Whole class

Take on the role of one of the characters introduced yesterday. Tell the children you are going to explain what happened to you and how you felt. Come out of role. Ask children in pairs to think of one question they would like to ask you. Go back into role and answer a selection of questions.

Group and independent work
In groups and using the same artefacts as yesterday as a stimulus, ask the children to think about what their character might say and how they might feel. Encourage children to discuss in pairs and take on the role of the character. They can record ideas on the second part of Copymaster 18.

Differentiation
Low Attainers – Use artefacts to act out dialogue from the story.
High Attainers – Pairs of children prepare a short dialogue between two characters in their story.

Lesson 3

Whole class

Cut Copymaster 19 into dialogue strips. Stick the second part of the utterances onto a board. Show the children the beginning of the utterances, one at a time, *e.g. 'Run, run as fast as you can . . .'* Ask the children to try to read it to themselves. (Low attainers may need help.) Show the children the second part of the utterances and ask them to match the strip. Encourage them to do this by reading to themselves first. Read the complete utterance and ask the children to identify the character and story.

Group and independent work

Give children the first part of different dialogue strips. Ask the children to copy these and write the second part of the utterance.

Differentiation

Low Attainers – Match two parts of dialogue strips and read to each other.

Whole class

Stick dialogue strips onto a board and read together with expression. Ask children to identify the character. List characters next to appropriate dialogue.

Lesson 4

Whole class

Tell the children that you are going to pretend to be a character from a traditional story. In role, tell the children about yourself. Come out of role and explain to the children that they are going to become this character. They are going to write a description of themselves for someone who has not seen or met them. Ask the children to think how they might begin in order to ensure the use of the first person and present tense. Use Copymaster 18 to model the beginning of a description, placing emphasis on the sentence structure.

Group and independent work

Children begin to write their character profiles.

Differentiation

Low Attainers – Children begin task orally and with adult support.
High Attainers – Write character profile without support.

Whole class

Children sit in a circle. Re-tell the story from the first part of the lesson around the group. Children take on the role of the character as the story is passed on. Encourage each child to make a contribution in role.

Lesson 5

Whole class

Choose examples of character profiles written in Lesson 4 to read with the class. Put onto OHT or enlarge for children to read. Pay particular attention to the use of the first person and present tense. Discuss and comment together where necessary. Strengthen vocabulary choices such as use of adjectives.

Group and independent work

Children complete written descriptions, correcting where necessary. Ask the children to use the description to illustrate their character.

Whole class

Encourage individual children to take on the role of their character as they read out their description. Display descriptions alongside illustrations.

Theme 2) Traditional stories – Little Red Riding Hood (week 1)

Objectives

Text level

- 1 To reinforce and apply word level skills through shared and guided reading;
- 5 To discuss story settings, to locate key words and phrases in text, to consider how different settings influence events and behaviour:
- 6 To identify and describe characters, expressing own views and using words and phrases from texts;
- 7 To prepare and re-tell stories individually through role-play in groups, using dialogue and narrative from text;
- 14 To write character profiles.

Resources

A collection of traditional stories.
A big book version of 'Little Red Riding Hood'.
Copymaster 20, Copymaster 21. Homework 12.

Resource preparation

Make a class display of traditional stories.
Enlarge a copy of Copymaster 20.

Assessment

At the end of this theme is the pupil able to:
- recognise how the setting in a story influences events and behaviour;
- write a character profile?

Lesson 1

Whole class

Explain to the children that the author of most traditional stories is unkown as they have been handed down through generations. Look at the front cover of the 'Little Red Riding Hood' text. If appropriate, draw the children's attention to the words 'retold by'. Explain this term to the children. Tell the children that they are going to have a go at re-telling the story before reading the book. Sit the children in a circle and ask them to re-tell a small part of the story each, whilst passing an object around the circle. Show the children an enlarged version of Copymaster 20. Tell them that they are going to choose their favourite traditional tale and describe it using the writing frame as a structure. Model part of this process for them, using the story of 'Little Red Riding Hood'.

Group and independent work

Ask the children to select their favourite traditional story and use the structure of the frame to describe it to the rest of the class.

Differentiation

Low Attainers – Re-tell the story of their favourite traditional story to an adult. Draw a picture of their favourite part of the story and write a sentence to describe it.
High Attainers – Encourage children to use the frame as sentence starters only. Can they think of an extra category to add to their frame?

Whole class

Ask some children to read selected parts from their work without telling the rest of the class the title of their chosen traditional story. Can they guess which story they are describing?

Lesson 2

Whole class

Begin by reading the whole story of 'Little Red Riding' Hood with the class. Ask the children to consider whether the author re-telling the story has added any of his or her own ideas to the story? Explain and discuss the term 'setting'. Ask the children to identify the settings in the story of 'Little Red Riding Hood' and make a list. Put the children into three groups and ask each group to brainstorm words to describe either the forest, Grandma's cottage or Little Red Riding Hood's house. Ask each group to feed back to the rest of the class. Discuss the reasons why each setting is the way it is, *e.g. the forest is spooky because the wolf is lurking in there.*

Group and independent work

Divide a piece of paper or a page in the children's books into three sections. Ask the children to draw and describe each of the settings in 'Little Red Riding Hood'. Can they re-tell one part of the story which takes place in that particular setting?

Differentiation

Low Attainers – Draw each of the settings and add descriptive words.
High Attainers – Ask children to give reasons as to why the illustrator has drawn that particular setting as it is.

Whole class

Organise children into pairs and give each pair a whiteboard. Ask them to write down one adjective to describe each setting. You may wish to ask some pairs to write more than one.

Lesson 3

Whole class

Ask the children to think about the character of the wolf in the story. Give pairs 'time out' to brainstorm words they would use to describe the wolf. These words can be recorded on whiteboards. Ask children to feed back to the rest of the class. Make a list of their descriptive words. Look through the book with the children and ask them to find words or phrases which describe the character of the wolf. Add these to the words on the class list.

Show the children an enlarged copy of Copymaster 21. Ask the children to imagine that the wolf is still on the loose and the police are trying to catch him. Tell the children that the police need them to make a 'wanted poster' which describes the wolf. Use shared writing to model this process for the children, encouraging the use of key words and phrases which could be used in a wanted poster, e.g. *This wolf is dangerous so don't approach him!*

Group and independent work

Children can produce their own wanted poster using the structure of Copymaster 21.

Differentiation

Low Attainers – Complete a similar poster with a picture of the wolf in the centre. Use repeating sentences to describe the wolf, beginning each sentence with, 'The wolf is …'

High Attainers – Encourage children to use full sentences in their posters using full stops and capital letters.

Whole class

Ask the children to pretend that the teacher is a TV presenter and they have been asked to appear on television to describe the wolf to the public. Interview selected children, asking them to use their posters to describe the wolf to the audience.

Lesson 4

Whole class

Recap on the children's descriptions of the wolf from the previous day. Tell the children that you are going to try to find out why the wolf acted the way he did in the story. Ask the children to imagine that they had the chance to interview the wolf to find out his reasons for tricking Little Red Riding Hood and eating Grandma. Give pairs 'time out' to allow the children to think of a question that they would like to ask the wolf if he was here. The teacher may want to take on the role of the wolf at this point to be able to explore the wolf's actions in more detail. Allow the children to ask their questions and during role-play try to establish reasons for the wolf's actions, e.g. *He had lost his way and was starving, another wolf had bullied him into capturing Grandma.* Try to make the character of the wolf remorseful, ready for group and independent work.

Group and independent work

Ask the children to pretend that they are the wolf and that they have to write a letter of apology to Little Red Riding Hood for the trouble they have caused. Encourage the children to use the reasons which emerged during role-play. Ask them to include a way in which the wolf will make it up to Little Red Riding Hood.

Differentiation

Low Attainers – Devise a letter as a group with an adult as scribe.

High Attainers – Ask children to set out the letter correctly, inventing an address for the wolf. Encourage them to think about how the wolf would be feeling at this point.

Whole class

Ask some children to read out their letters taking on the characteristics of the wolf. Discuss the effectiveness of the letters.

Lesson 5

Whole class

Tell the children that today you are going to try to establish the thoughts and feelings of Little Red Riding Hood. Ask the children to think about how Little Red Riding Hood might have felt when she discovered that her Grandma was really the wolf. Ask the children to show you using facial expressions. Ask the children to think of questions they could ask Little Red Riding Hood to try to find out her feelings towards the wolf. List these. Put the children into pairs and ask one child to take on the role of the interviewer and one to be Little Red Riding Hood. Ask the interviewer to use the listed questions to try to find out how Little Red Riding Hood feels. Ask the children who were the interviewers to feed back to the rest of the class.

Group and independent work

Ask the children to write another letter but this time as if they were Little Red Riding Hood. Tell them that they are replying to the wolf and they may decide to forgive him or they might still be angry with him.

Differentiation

Low Attainers – This could again be completed as a group with an adult scribe if appropriate. The children may want to role-play Little Red Riding Hood's response in pairs.

High Attainers – Encourage children to set their letter out correctly using an address for Little Red Riding Hood. Encourage them to think carefully about Little Red Riding Hood's character when writing their letter.

Whole class

Put the children into pairs and ask one to take on the role of the wolf and one to be Little Red Riding Hood. Ask them to use their letters to role-play the situation where the wolf tries to apologise to Little Red Riding Hood. Ask the children to feed back on their conversations to the rest of the class.

Theme 3) Traditional stories – Little Red Riding Hood (Week 2)

Objectives

Text level
- 12 Through shared and guided writing to apply phonological, graphic knowledge and sight vocabulary to spell words accurately;
- 13 To use story settings from reading in their own writing.

Sentence level
- 3 To re-read own writing to check for grammatical sense and accuracy – identify errors and suggest alternative constructions;
- 4 To be aware of the need for grammatical agreement in speech and writing, matching verbs to nouns/pronouns correctly.

Resources
A range of traditional tales.
Copymaster 22, Copymaster 23, Copymaster 24.
Homework 13.

Assessment
At the end of this theme is the pupil able to:
- use the setting and structure of Little Red Riding Hood to construct their own story ending;
- use grammatical agreement correctly in speech and writing;
- re-read their own writing to check for grammatical sense and accuracy and suggest the appropriate corrections?

Lesson 1

Whole class

Begin this week by recapping on, or introducing, the term 'verb' to the children. Put the children into pairs and give each pair a whiteboard and marker. Ask the pairs to write down a verb on their whiteboard. Tell the children that they can check whether their word is a verb by putting the word 'to' in front of it to see if it makes sense, *e.g. to jump, to go*. Make a class list of all the verbs produced in this activity. Enlarge the sentences on Copymaster 22 or write them onto the class board. Tell the children that you have been trying to remember parts of the story of 'Little Red Riding Hood' and have written these out in sentences. Ask the children if they would like to check your sentences for you. Read the first sentence with the children. Ask them to identify the word which is incorrect. Can they give you the correct word? Explain to the children that often the verb in a sentence has to change to ensure that the sentence makes sense. This depends on whether there is one or more people in the sentence. Correct the first two or three sentences with the children.

Group and independent work
Ask the children to read the remaining sentences on Copymaster 22 with a partner. Can they find the word which is incorrect? Ask them to copy out the sentences using the corrected word.

Differentiation
Low Attainers – Give the group a few of the sentences written out onto a large sheet of paper. The children can cover the incorrect word with a piece of paper and write the correct word onto it. They may need some support with the reading of the sentences.
High Attainers – Make up five sentences which do not make sense, i.e. the grammatical agreement is incorrect. Swap these sentences with a friend and correct each other's sentences.

Whole class
Ask the high attainers to read out some of the incorrect sentences to the class. You may need to write these up. Can the rest of the children identify the incorrect word and give the correct one?

Lesson 2

Whole class

Explain to the children that most traditional stories are written in a similar way and will use similar words and phrases. Ask the children if anyone knows a common opening sentence for a traditional story? Show the children some traditional stories from the class collection and read the first line. Make a class list of common ways that traditional stories begin. Repeat this with endings to traditional stories. Ask the children to comment on the things that they notice about these endings, *e.g. they are always happy*. Skim read the big book of Little Red Riding Hood with the children and look for any other key features of traditional stories or common words and phrases which are used.

Group and independent work
Put the children into groups and give each group a selection of traditional tales. Ask the children to record any different beginnings, endings or key words or phrases onto a large piece of sugar paper.

Differentiation
This activity is an opportunity for the children to work in mixed ability groups. It is a good idea to assign a more able child in the group to be the scribe.

Whole class
Ask the groups to report back on their findings, nominating one child as their spokesperson. Add any new findings to the class list. Display this as a reference poster.

Lesson 3

Whole class

Tell the children that over the next few days you are going to re-write the ending of 'Little Red Riding Hood'. Ask the children to think about the character of the woodcutter at the end of the story. Do the children think that he is a good hero for children of today, or could they invent a better one for the story? Discuss the children's views on this. Tell the children that they are going to have a go at inventing a new hero for the story of 'Little Red Riding Hood'. Show the children an enlarged version of Copymaster 23. Model the process of inventing a hero using this structure. Remind the children the book is written for young children so we don't want to frighten them. They also need to ensure that their character fits in with the story, *e.g. it could be an animal from the forest or Little Red Riding Hood's mum turning into Super mum!*

Group and independent work

Ask the children to invent their own hero to replace the character of the woodcutter in 'Little Red Riding Hood' using the structure of Copymaster 23. Make sure that they list their hero's special features and describe how he/she will save Grandma from the wolf.

Differentiation

Low Attainers – Draw a picture of their new super hero and label his/her key features.
High Attainers – Encourage this group to think carefully about the adjectives they select when describing their hero, thinking about the qualities which make heroes in other stories or television programmes.

Whole class

Ask the children to introduce their new super hero to the class. Focus on how the hero is going to save Grandma.

Lesson 4

Whole class

Begin by telling the children that today they are going to write their character into the story of Little Red Riding Hood. Tell the children that they are only re-writing the end of the story using the character which they have invented instead of the woodcutter. Give the children a starter for the end of their story, *e.g. 'All the better to eat you with,' snarled the wolf*. Use the shared writing process to write an ending to the story. Use the hero that was created by the class in Lesson 3 for the shared piece. Remind the children of the list of key words and phrases that was generated in Lesson 2.

Group and independent work

Ask the children to write a new ending to the story of Little Red Riding Hood, using the hero that they created yesterday. Encourage the children to write in sentences using full stops and capital letters and to use the bank of words and phrases generated during Lesson 3.

Differentiation

Low Attainers – This activity can be completed using a storyboard format with four boxes. The children can draw four pictures and write sentences underneath with adult support if appropriate.
High Attainers – Encourage this group to think carefully about their use of descriptive phrases. Encourage the use of connectives to join sentences.

Whole class

Put the children into pairs and ask them to read three or four lines of their new ending to their partner. Ask some children to comment on one thing they liked about their partner's writing.

Lesson 5

Whole class

Tell the children that you have written your own version of the end of the Little Red Riding Hood story and that you would like them to check your work for you. Show the children an enlarged copy of Copymaster 24. Read this through with the children and ask them to show you a sign when they spot something which isn't correct (*e.g. put your finger on your nose*). Ask the children to identify the word and give you the correct word to replace it. When you have finished this, read through the whole passage with the children to check that it makes sense. Put the children into pairs. Ask each child to read their story endings to a friend. Tell the children that when they have listened to their friend's story they have to comment on their favourite part and then find one word that needs correcting. Ask pairs to feed back on their findings to the rest of the class.

Group and independent work

Having read their work aloud, ask the children to read through their work again and correct any mistakes which they can see. Encourage the children to look for simple spellings, grammatical agreement and overall sense. Ask the children to write out their final draft when their mistakes have been corrected. These can be completed on paper and put into a class book.

Differentiation

High Attainers – Ask this group to look for places where two sentences can be joined. Encourage them to select connectives other than 'and'. Remind them to check their use of punctuation.

Whole class

Ask some children to present their finished endings to the class. Encourage the other children to say what they liked about that story and to give reasons for their answers.

Theme 4 Traditional stories from other cultures (week 1)

Objectives

Text level
- 4 To predict incidents from text;
- 6 To identify and describe characters using words and phrases from the text;
- 14 To write character profiles using key words and phrases that describe, or are spoken by, characters in the text.

Sentence level
- 6 To identify speech marks in reading, understand their purpose and use the term correctly.

Word level
- 11 To use antonyms: correct and discuss differences of meaning and their spelling.

Resources
A collection of traditional tales from a range of cultures. 'The King with Dirty Feet' from 'The King with Dirty Feet and other stories' compiled by Mary Medlicott.

Enlarged copies of Copymaster 25 and Copymaster 26. Copymaster 26 with speech marks deleted. Three column grid for listing characters. Homework 14.

Resource preparation
Begin to set up a class display to which children can contribute personal copies of traditional stories.

Assessment
At the end of this theme is the pupil able to:
- identify, describe and compare characters in relation to the text and their own ideas;
- identify direct speech in reading;
- write dialogue using speech bubbles;
- present work to the class?

Lesson 1

Whole class

Introduce this unit of work by making a list of traditional stories known to the class. Make use of the 'time out' strategy in order for children to discuss in pairs traditional stories they know.
Draw attention to the display of traditional stories.
Explain that during the unit you will be looking at traditional stories from other cultures.
Introduce the focus text. Read the beginning together using an enlarged version of Copymaster 25.
Ask the children if they notice any similarities with other traditional stories they know.
Consider the language features as well as content. Make a list of responses.

Group and independent work
Using the display and their own knowledge, ask children to make a list of their three favourite traditional stories and give reasons for their choices.

Differentiation
Low Attainers – Tell children to listen to a taped version of a well known story and follow the text.
High Attainers – Ask children to look at how five traditional stories begin and end and make a list on a large piece of paper.

Whole class
Individual children can give reasons for choosing their favourite traditional story.
A group can share their examples of openings and endings.

Lesson 2

Whole class

Read the second page of the story in the book to the class (p 5). Ask the children to predict what may happen next.
Read the next page together using Copymaster 26.
Divide the class. One half reads the king's dialogue and the other Gabu's dialogue. The teacher can read indirect/reported speech.
In pairs, children take the role of the king and Gabu and read together trying to leave out reported speech.
Discuss the role of speech marks around direct speech.
Compose a one sentence prompt sheet to help children to remember when to use speech marks.

Group and independent work
Ask the children to prepare, rehearse and read onto tape the dialogue between the king and Gabu.
Discuss in pairs and list three things that could happen next in the story.

Differentiation
Low Attainers – Role-play the story so far.
High Attainers – Use Copymaster 26 with speech marks deleted and try to replace them.

Whole class
Listen to taped versions and watch the role play.
Compare the different versions.
Ask the children what they think may happen next.
Make brief notes for Lesson 3.

Lesson 3

Whole class

Read to the end of the story and compare events with those predicted by the children in Lesson 2.
Name the three main characters and list on a board.
Organise a 'show me' activity with whiteboards where children write characteristics of the king and the old man. Use a grid with three columns to list characteristics suggested by the children of the King, the old man and Gabu.
Refer back to the text where appropriate.
Highlight the differences between the two characters and draw attention to antonyms, e.g. the king was stupid, the old man was clever.

Group and independent work

Use a three column grid and list characteristics of the king and the old man using ideas from shared work and own ideas. List characteristics of Gabu in column three.

Differentiation

Low Attainers – Draw your favourite character from the story and write words to describe them around the picture.
High Attainers – Using the list generated in whole class work as a starting point, make an individual antonym list. How many can you think of?

Whole class

Compare characteristics of Gabu with the other two characters.

Lesson 4

Whole class

Using large speech bubbles drawn onto a board or paper, compose the beginning of a dialogue between the king and the old man. Think back to other traditional stories and what the king might offer the old man for his help. What would be the old man's response?
Relate the speech bubbles to dialogue read earlier in the week, particularly highlighting the lack of reported speech with speech bubbles. You may wish to develop this by comparing with a text where speech bubbles are included.

Group and independent work

Write a speech bubble dialogue, e.g. between the king and Gabu or between two characters from another well known traditional story.

Differentiation

Low Attainers – Use finger or stick puppets to help compose dialogue. An adult could write for children if necessary. Use a page from a familiar traditional tale to add speech bubbles.
High Attainers – Before they start to write their speech bubble dialogue, think about the characteristics of their chosen characters and how that would influence what they say.

Whole class

Read a selection of dialogues with appropriate expression.

Lesson 5

Whole class

Use enlarged examples of children's speech bubble dialogue and:
• read together;
• improve the content and choice of vocabulary;
• edit in relation to spelling errors;
• re-read together.
Make these stages clear to the children by writing them on a board as you do them.

Group and independent work

Ask children to draft and edit their speech bubble dialogues in the same way as in the whole class activity. Tell them to use the steps listed on the board as a guide.

Differentiation

Low Attainers – Prepare dialogue using puppets with text written in Lesson 4.
High Attainers – Work with a partner to improve dialogue and prepare for presentation.

Whole class

Present work to the class.
Encourage children to reflect on the theme, e.g.:
• Did they like the story? Why?
• Were the characters and events is the story similar to those in traditional stories they already know?

Texts and activities in weeks 2 and 3 are linked. Suggested texts have been used in the weekly units of work. However, any two traditional stories with the same themes could be used.

Objectives

Text level
* 5 To discuss story settings to compare differences, to locate key words and phrases in text;
* 13 To use story settings from reading.

Sentence level
* 9 To secure the use of simple sentences in own writing.

Word level
* 10 To build individual collections of significant words.

Resources
'How Rabbit Stole the Fire: A North American Indian folk tale' by Joanna Troughton.

'Rainbow Bird: An Aboriginal folk tale from Northern Australia' by Eric Maddern and Adrienne Kennaway.
1 Blank tape.
Homework 15.

Resource preparation
A collection of pictures or postcards from a range of different settings.

Assessment
At the end of this theme is the pupil able to:
* discuss and compare story settings;
* write descriptions of settings from reading?

Lesson 1

Whole class

Explain to the class that they will be looking at two similar stories that take place in different settings. Ask children to think back to the previous text 'The King with Dirty Feet', and where that story took place. Show the children the first double page spread illustration in 'Rainbow Bird'. Ask the children to work in pairs and tell one child to describe the scene to a partner. Write contributions from children around the picture on paper or a board.
Read 'Rainbow Bird' and ask children to listen for words/phrases that describe the setting, *e.g. 'cold at night'*. Record your reading of the book onto tape.

Group and independent work
Using traditional stories from the class display, ask children to choose a story, look at the illustrations and find words or phrases in the text which describe the setting.

Differentiation
Low Attainers – Listen to taped version of 'Rainbow Bird'. Look at the book and list 5 words to describe the setting.
High Attainers – Select challenging texts.

Whole class
Children read out words and phrases describing settings and the class try to guess the story from the traditional story display. Select words and phrases and make a list to describe settings. Read the list together.

Lesson 2

Whole class

Without any discussion, read 'How Rabbit Stole the Fire'. Ask the children to think about similarities with 'Rainbow Bird', i.e. importance of fire. Ask children where they think 'How Rabbit Stole the Fire' takes place. Show the illustration from the first double page spread. In the same pairs as yesterday, children describe the setting. Take feedback and write words/phrases onto paper or a board around the picture. Read the words/phrases together. Pick two examples and ask children if they can think of a better word or phrase, *e.g. a stronger adjective*.

Group and independent work
Give the children an A4 sheet of paper with a postcard or a picture of a setting secured onto it. Ask the children to think of five words or phrases to describe their setting. Tell children to write their first ideas in pencil then re-read and rethink their choice of words, adding to phrases and changing words using a different colour pencil or felt-tip pen. This activity may be carried out in pairs or small groups.

Differentiation
Low Attainers – Listen to the taped version of 'How Rabbit Stole the Fire'. Make a list of the animals in the story.
High Attainers – Children add to and improve description from whole class work.

Whole class
Read and compare words and phrases from whole class work in Lessons 1 and 2. Ask the children which setting they prefer and why.

Lesson 3

Whole class

Using words and phrases generated in Lesson 2, model the first sentence of a description of the setting of 'Rainbow Bird'. Give children 'time out' in pairs to compose sentences. Discuss appropriate sentence punctuation. Re-read together and improve word choices.

Group and independent work
Give children the first sentence from 'How Rabbit Stole the Fire'.
'In the beginning there was no fire on Earth, and the world was cold.'

Ask children to write a description in sentences about the setting using words and phrases collected in Lesson 2.

Differentiation
Low Attainers – Write a group description of the setting. write for the group if necessary.
High Attainers – Ask children to add some new descriptive phrases and words. Ask children to add one sentence of their own.

Whole class
Re-read the shared text from whole class work. Read shared text from low attaining group. Compare the two descriptions. Ask the children to pick one phrase from each text which gives an overall picture of the setting.

Lesson 4

Whole class

Take examples of children's work and put onto OHT or write onto large pieces of paper (ask their permission first).
Read together. Give the children 'time out' to find a descriptive phrase they like. Pick one word or phrase and ask children to think of a more appropriate word. Take some examples from the children and substitute the most popular. Ask the children to find one example of a spelling or punctuation error. Choose two or three examples and demonstrate how to edit the writing.

Group and independent work
Ask children to re-read their own work and compare

with a partner's work. Tell children to find one good thing about each piece of work and one thing that could be improved.

Differentiation
Low Attainers – Copy the shared text written in Lesson 3. Ask each child to add one more sentence.
High Attainers – Look carefully at the descriptions. Use a thesaurus to find more interesting words.

Whole class
Children sit in a circle. Ask pairs to discuss one of the changes they made and why.

Lesson 5

Whole class

Tell children that they are going to make a best copy of their work and illustrate the setting. Talk about the required format, *e.g. layout, care with full stops and capital letters, importance of checking spellings they are unsure of.*

Group and independent work
Children prepare best copy for a display or book form and illustrate.

Differentiation
Low Attainers – Check work completed during Lesson 4,

re-read and illustrate paying close attention to the description.
High Attainers – Encourage children to pay close attention to changes for their finished piece of work.

Whole class
Children sit in a circle with their finished work. Ask for volunteers to read their work to the rest of the class. Ask children which setting they preferred, North America or Australia. Which one would they like to visit and why?

Theme 6 Traditional stories from other cultures (week 3)

Objectives

Text level
• 13 To use story setting from reading to write a different story in the same setting.

Sentence level
• 3 To re-read own writing to check for grammatical sense and accuracy, identify errors and suggest alternative constructions.

Word level
• 10 To use new words from reading.

Resources
Work on settings from previous week.
Copymasters 27, 28 and 29. Homework 16.

Assessment
At the end of this theme is the pupil able to:
• write a new story in the setting described previously;
• re-read ongoing work and suggest improvements at text, sentence and word level?

Lesson 1

Whole class

Explain to the class that this week they are going to write their own stories based on 'How Rabbit Stole the Fire', using the setting they described last week. Completed stories will be read onto tape.
Remind the children of the repetitive nature of 'How Rabbit Stole the Fire':
• when deciding who could steal the fire;
• when rabbit was chased by the Sky People;
• when the animals were passing the fire.
Use Copymaster 27 to begin planning a story with the whole class. Use note form, not whole sentences. Ask children to think of a good start to the story. Remind them that they can refer to the setting. Write a first sentence on a board. Re-read with the children.

Group and independent work
Children use Copymaster 27 to plan their story and write the first sentence.

Differentiation
Low Attainers – With adult support children read through the plan from shared text work.
High Attainers – Think how they can incorporate a description of the setting in the first sentence.
An adult supports the group in turning the plan into an oral story and makes additional notes from children's contributions.

Whole class
Children share their opening sentences. Comment on appropriate opening phrases and the use of setting descriptions.

Lesson 2

Whole class

Use the opening sentences from Lesson 1 and compose with the class the next part of the story. Refer to story plans produced in Lesson 1 in order to incorporate appropriate characters. Re-read together, checking punctuation. Look for alternative word choices and decide on the best. Focus particularly on high attainers for response. Tell children they are going to continue with writing their story up to the point where the other animals helped to steal the fire. Tell the children to re-read their story plan before they start.

Group and independent work
Children add to the first sentences produced yesterday.

Teacher and other adult help encourage the children to sequence events orally before they start to write, using their story plans from Lesson 1 to help.

Differentiation
Low Attainers – Use Copymaster 28 to complete the sentences and illustrate boxes 1 and 2 and write the first part of their story independently.
High Attainers – Work independently using story plan for guidance.

Whole class
High attainers read their work to group. Encourage children to comment on something they liked about the work.

Lesson 3

Whole class

Write on the board or put onto OHT an example of one child's work from Lesson 2. Ask the child's permission first.
Read together. Ask the child how he/she intends to continue the story. Ask the rest of the class to comment on ideas and make suggestions. Ask the class to think about a repetitive phrase that could be used to structure events and writing. Write up suggestions as prompts for the whole class. Nominate 3 children to read their work in the plenary.

Group and independent work

Children continue their story writing but not to complete the ending.

Differentiation

Low Attainers – Ask children to read work produced on Copymaster 28 in Lesson 2. Tell them to complete boxes 3, 4 and 5 with adult help, if available.
High Attainers – Work with the teacher to read and discuss work in progress, paying particular attention to grammatical sense and accuracy.

Whole class

Ask the nominated three children to read their work in progress. Encourage the rest of the class to comment on something they liked about the writing.

Lesson 4

Whole class

Read the last page of 'How Rabbit Stole the Fire'. Discuss the ending. Read the last page of 'Rainbow Bird'. Discuss the ending and compare with 'How Rabbit Stole the Fire'. Use Copymaster 29 to highlight features of endings of the two stories and make general points about the endings of traditional stories. Highlight what happened to the characters in both stories. On a board write phrases from the final pages:
• 'And to this day ...'
• 'And Rainbow Bird?'
• 'Now the animals have fire ...'
Discuss how the children can use these techniques in their endings, ie.:
• linking the story to the present
• telling the reader what happened to the main character
• summing up the events.

Group and independent work

Children complete their stories paying particular attention to the earlier discussion.

Differentiation

Low Attainers – Encourage children to read work from Copymaster 28 to an adult. Discuss how children can complete box 6 and support children writing their story endings.
High Attainers – Complete story ending and read to a partner. Refer to points made on Copymaster 29 in whole class work. Make sure the endings of the stories are appropriate.

Lesson 5

Whole class

Use examples of children's work on OHT or written onto a board to discuss:
• the use of sentence punctuation;
• the spelling of high frequency words and long vowel choices.
Re-read sentences together. Ask children if full stops and capital letters are in the right place. Ask children to spot incorrect spellings and try to write the correct spelling on a whiteboard. Support low attainers.

Group and independent work

Children finish writing and illustrating their stories and check their punctuation and spelling.

Whole class

Children sit in a circle. Evaluate the writing activity. Ask the children what they liked about the writing task and what they found difficult. Use adult support to re-read work with individual children. Check the use of punctuation in re-reading.

Theme 7) Poems with predictable and patterned language

For this unit you may be able to find poems with predictable and patterned language from other cultures.

Objectives

Text level
* 9 To identify and discuss patterns in rhythm and rhyme in different poems;
* 10 To comment on and recognise when the reading aloud of a poem makes sense and is effective;
* 11 To identify and discuss favourite poems, referring to the language of the poem;
* 15 To use structures from poems as a basis for writing, by extending and substituting elements;
* 2 To read aloud with intonation and expression appropriate to the grammar and punctuation.

Word level
* 4 To split familiar oral and written compound words into their component parts;
* 5 To discriminate orally syllables in multi-syllabic words from reading, extend to written forms and note syllable boundary in speech and writing.

Resources
'Morning' by Grace Nichols (Copymaster 30).
A collection of poems or poetry books containing poems by authors from a range of cultures e.g. 'Give Yourself a Hug' by Grace Nichols, 'I Like That Stuff – poems from many cultures' selected by Morag Styles, 'Skip across the Ocean' by Floella Benjamin. Copymaster 31. Homework 17.

Assessment:
At the end of this theme is the pupil able to:
* discuss a selected poem, referring to the language of the poem;
* read poems aloud with intonation and expression;
* use the structure from the poem as a basis for writing;
* show an awareness of syllables in words and use an appropriate number of syllables in written phrases;
* show an awareness of compound words, identify in reading and generate some of their own?

Lesson 1

Whole class

Refer to Autumn Term poetry work. Ask the children if they can remember titles of poems that were read and used in class and any of the poets. Make a list on the board.
Ask children if anyone has another favourite poem and why they like it. Read 'Morning' Copymaster 30. Give children 'time out' to read the poem themselves. (Give low attainers adult support for re-reading) Ask the children which verse reminds them most of their morning time. Ask the children about the form of the poem. Collect ideas drawing out:
* repetitive first line;
* lack of punctuation;
* the title is the first word in every line;
* the structure of the last verse is different.

Group and independent work
Ask children to choose a poem from the class collection. Ask pairs of children to read their chosen poems together, choose two phrases from the poem that they like and note 3 things about the shape, rhyme or pattern of the poem. Tell children to record their observations on Copymaster 31.

Lesson 2

Whole class

Write on a large sheet of paper phrases from the poem 'Morning', e.g. 'milk-float jiggling', 'milkman whistling', 'empties clinking', 'alarm-clock ringing'. Read the phrases with the children, clapping the syllables. Ask the children if they can see a pattern. (4 syllables in each phrase, 2 syllables in each word.)
Give the children the beginning of each of the following similar phrases and ask them to think of ways of completing the phrase, e.g. 'brown dog …', 'baby …', 'bath-tap …', 'tractor …'. Add ideas to the list and then clap the syllables to check the pattern.
Read the phrases together keeping a strict rhythm. Ask groups of children to read the phrases aloud to the rest of the class.

Group and independent work
Think of second words to the following: 'blackbirds …..', 'postman …', 'TV …', 'sunshine …', 'Corn Flakes …'. Ask the children to add two new complete phrases of their own.

Differentiation
Low Attainers – Write the first words of some phrases onto whiteboards and ask the children to write the second word of the phrase. Stress 'ing' endings.
High Attainers – How many whole phrases can you compose?

Whole class
Write the given first words onto a board. Ask children for some second words to complete the phrases. Discuss alternatives, substituting until everyone is happy with the phrase. Read through together.

Lesson 3

Whole class

Give pairs of children a whiteboard and pen. Tell them to write 'Morning comes' on their board. Write the 2 words on a large board and tell the children to check to see if they have written it correctly. Using the 'time out' strategy, ask pairs to discuss and then write the next line of the poem. Refer to, but do not show the children, the phrases composed yesterday. Support low attainers through discussion and write if necessary. Ask children to sit in a circle. Ask pairs to read out verses around the circle.

Group and independent work

In a group (3 pairs) ask children to put their whiteboards on the table and read the three verses together. Each pair then writes another verse. Children can continue to use whiteboards for composition, but then transfer their work onto paper. Each child should have four verses, three of which may be the same as other group members.

Differentiation

Low Attainers – Write out the three verses from whiteboards to make their own poems.
High Attainers – Discuss the group examples. Look at word choices and think of more appropriate or alternative choices.

Whole class

Low attainers read their poems to the rest of the class.

Lesson 4

Whole class

Return to 'Morning'. Look at the last verse. Discuss who 'Boss Woman' could be. Discuss the expression and whether the children or their families might use it. This could lead to discussion about use of dialect in poems. Some children may have examples from their independent reading. Ask children if and how they might want to change that last line to finish their poems. Write some examples on the board and read together. *e.g. Busy Mum Morning, Time for School Morning.*

Group and independent work

In pairs complete a last verse for the poem written yesterday. Read through and check spellings. Write the poem out individually.

Differentiation

Low Attainers – Add a last verse to the poem written yesterday. Use the ideas and work generated in the whole class session.

Whole class

Read some examples of final verses.

Lesson 5

Whole class

Ask children to look at 'Morning' and find a word that can be split into two words. They may point out 'milk-float', 'milkman', and 'alarm-clock'. Discuss the use of the hyphen and that it is a punctuation mark that links two words or parts of words. (Use the glossary in the NLS Framework for teaching for more detail.) Write 'milkman' on the board. Refer to the list of phrases generated in Lesson 2. Pick out other compound words and add to the list. Tell the children that this is called a compound word. (A word made of two other words.) Write 'Compound Words' on the board and ask the children to think of a definition for a compound word. Write ideas on the board, ending up with one sentence above the compound words generated.

Group and independent work

• Copy from the board the heading Compound Words, the definition, and the examples generated in whole class work. This will form the basis of the homework.
• With a partner read poems from Lesson 1. Look for examples of compound words and add to the list.
• Finish copying out poems from Lesson 4.

Differentiation

Low Attainers – Give children some cut up compound words and ask them to put them together, *e.g. football, hairbrush, bathroom, bedroom.*
High Attainers – Add to the words 'any' and 'some' to make as many compound words as you can.

Whole class

Orally collect additional compound words. Do not add to the list as children can do this at home.

Theme 8   Poems with predictable and patterned language

Objectives
Text level
- 8 To read poems aloud;
- 9 To identify and discuss patterns of rhythm;
- 10 To comment on and recognise when the reading aloud of a poem makes sense and is effective;
- 15 To use structures from poems as a basis for writing by substituting elements and inventing own lines.

Resources
'I'm just going out for a moment' by Michael Rosen from 'Poems Not To Be Missed' chosen by Susan Hill and Debby Strauss (Copymaster 32).
'My Sweet' by Richard Brown from 'A Lick of the Spoon' poems chosen by Richard Brown and Kate Ruttle (Copymaster 34).
Both poems cut up into lines for ordering.
Copymasters 32, 33, 34 and Copymaster 35.
Homework 18.

Assessment
At the end of this theme is the pupil able to:
- discuss patterns in poems;
- read poems aloud and comment on when the reading is effective;
- write own poems based on those read?

Lesson 1
Whole class

Tell the children that this week you are going to look at two poems and use the poems as a structure to help them write their own. Ask them if they can remember some poems that they have read before and who wrote them. Read to the children 'I'm just going out for a moment' (Copymaster 32). Re-read the poem, asking the children to join in. Ask the children what they think the poem is about. Some might have younger brothers and sisters who are always asking 'Why?'. Read again with half of the class reading the statement and the other half reading the question. Give the children 'time out' in pairs to discuss the pattern of the poem. Draw attention to the rhythm and read once again.

Group and independent work
Cut the poem on Copymaster 32 into strips and ask children to put it in the correct order and stick it onto paper. You may want certain groups to have some of the poem already in place.

Differentiation
Low Attainers – Re-read the poem with the children. Encourage children to read different parts of the poem. Prepare a presentation for the plenary.
High Attainers – Give children the whole poem to sort.

Whole class
Low attaining children present their version of the poem to the rest of the class. Comment on the use of expression and how the poem was read.

Lesson 2
Whole class

Use an enlarged version of Copymaster 32. Read the first two lines. Ask the children to think of another reason for going out for a moment, *e.g. to make a sandwich, to feed the cat.* List their responses. Take one example and continue writing the next two lines together.

Group and independent work
Give children the writing frame Copymaster 33 and ask them to write their own version of the poem, using ideas from the list produced in the whole class session.

Differentiation
Low Attainers – Children could either:
- continue writing the poem started in the whole class session;
- work on a version of the poem with only two lines missing and complete; or
- work with adult support using the writing frame on Copymaster 33.
High Attainers – Write their own poems without the support of the writing frame.

Whole class
Ask some children to read their poems to the rest of the class. Pick children to comment on the poems.

Lesson 3

Whole class

Read 'My Sweet' to the class without them seeing the text. Ask the children how the poem starts and ends, i.e. with a question. Read the poem on an enlarged version of Copymaster 34 together. Draw attention to the sequence:

When you first pop it in . . .
And when you start to chew . . .
And when you swallow my sweet . . .

Look at the way in which the lines are broken up in the poem and compare with 'I'm just going out for a moment'.

Talk about how you should read certain phrases:
e.g. 'your arms go Zing!
and your legs go Zong!'

Reread the poem together, putting in expression.

Group and independent work

As in Lesson 1, give the children the poem cut into lines and ask them to reassemble the poem with a partner.

Differentiation

Low Attainers – An adult works with children using 'My Sweet' poem with words missing. Support the children in reading the poem together and placing words in the correct place. Discuss and re-read.

High Attainers – Encourage children to re-read for sense and make sure they start a new line in the correct place.

Whole class

Ask the children to read 'I'm just going out for a moment' and 'My Sweet' aloud, putting in the appropriate expression. Give them minimal support. Praise good use of expression.

Lesson 4

Whole class

Read 'My Sweet' with the whole class. Give the children a sweet. Show children Copymaster 35. Tell them to put their sweet in their mouths and think how they feel. Take some ideas from the children. Write three or four examples on the board and then choose the best to put into the poem. Write the verse beginning 'When you first pop it in.'

Tell the children that they are going to continue writing the poem, but not to start to chew the sweet until they are in their places!

Group and independent work

Children write their own versions of the poem using Copymaster 35.

Differentiation

Low Attainers – Give children a more detailed version of Copymaster 35, depending on the level of support they need. This could be the poem with some words missing.

High Attainers – Give children support in developing their poems. Discuss ideas and choice of words. Encourage children to re-read their work as they write.

Whole class

Sit children in a circle and give them 'time out' to discuss which poem they prefer from the two you have been reading this week. Tell them to think of two reasons for their preference. Share and compare ideas.

Lesson 5

Whole class

Pre-select 2 versions of 'My Sweet' written by the children, ask the children's permission and enlarge. Ask the writers to read their poem, or read it yourself to the class. Ask children to make a comment about the content. Does the poem make them feel they would like to eat that sweet? Look at layout and organisation, particularly where children have started a new line. Discuss any changes that could be made.

Give out versions of poems children have written this week. Tell the children that they must:
• read any comments and corrections on the work;
• decide which poem they want to write out in their best handwriting for a class display.

Group and independent work

Children copy out their chosen poem for display and illustrate.

Differentiation

Low Attainers – Their poems will look more like the originals. Children could work with a partner and copy out half the poem. Give adult support to ensure they have a suitable finished product.

High Attainers – Tell children to look carefully at comments on the poems and act on them with regard to the composition before they copy out the poem.

Whole class

Put work on the tables around the room. Ask children to look at the poems. You may be able to persuade another adult to visit and look at the work. Come back together and comment on the work.

Set up homework by giving children a copy of a rhyming poem. Choose appropriate poems for different groups of children.

Theme 9) Explanations

Objectives

Text level
- 19 To read flow charts and cyclical diagrams which explain a process;
- 21 To produce simple flow charts or diagrams that explain a process.

Resources
A collection of texts or text extracts which contain examples of explanation. These examples should explain why or how something happens, *e.g. Dorling Kindersley 'Why' series*. These books explain a range of subjects which interest children.
Copymaster 36, Copymaster 37. Homework 19.

Resource preparation
Set up a class display of examples of explanation texts and extracts.
Photocopy three enlarged examples of explanations including one which uses a diagram or flow chart (life-cycles are a good example of this) ready for whole class sessions. Enlarge and cut up Copymaster 37.

Assessment
At the end of this theme is the pupil able to:
- read and follow a simple flow chart or diagram which explains a process;
- produce their own simple flow chart or diagram which explains a process?

Lesson 1

Whole class

Begin by asking the children if anyone knows what a question is. Ask for a volunteer to come to the front and ask you a question beginning with 'how' or 'why'. Ask the rest of the class if the volunteer has asked a question. Write the given question on the board, reinforcing the use of a question mark at the end of the sentence. Put children into pairs. Ask each child to think of a simple question to ask their partner. Encourage the children to answer their partner's question using a complete sentence. Ask each pair to tell the class their question and answer. Focus on the answers to the questions ensuring that the children are answering in complete sentences. Model answering the question on the board using some complete sentences, *e.g. What is your name? My name is …*
Using the children's questions from their work in pairs, write a series of questions on the board for the children to answer. *e.g. How old are you? Why do you wear glasses?*

How do you travel to school? etc. Tell the children that their answers to the questions are the start of explanations and that you will be looking at texts that explain things during the week.

Group and independent work
Ask the children to write each question and answer them in complete sentences. Remind the children to use questions marks in their work.

Differentiation
Low Attainers – Ask this group to ask each other questions orally, answering in complete sentences.
High Attainers – Encourage children to invent their own questions to answer. Ask them to write three questions for a partner to answer, then swap their work with a friend.

Whole class
Ask some children to read the answers to their questions. Focus on whether the children have answered the questions using complete sentences.

Lesson 2

Whole class

Tell the children that you are going to look at explanation texts this week. Explain to them that an explanation answers a question and explains how or why something happens. Use an enlarged example of an explanation for whole class shared reading. Ask the children what they notice about the text. Is it set out like a story? How is it different? What features has the author used to help them explain something to the reader, *e.g. bold text, pictures and diagrams?* Begin to make a class list of these words. Look at the second example of an explanation and discuss the key features of the text and the language used. Ask the children to identify any similar features and add any new ones to the class list.

Group and independent work
Put the children into small groups and give each group a selection of explanation texts. Using a large sheet of paper, ask them to record the subject that the various texts are explaining, any key features which are used and the language which is used to begin sentences.

Differentiation
This is an opportunity for the children to work in mixed ability pairs. You may want to ensure that a more able child acts as the scribe for their group.

Whole class
Ask the groups to report back on their findings. Add any new features which have been identified to the class list.

Lesson 3
Whole class

Tell the children that today they are going to write their own explanation. Ask the children to imagine that they have met an alien who doesn't know anything about earth and doesn't understand why humans wear clothes. Put the children into pairs and ask each pair to think of one reason which explains why we need to wear clothes. Make a class brainstorm of their answers. Tell the children that they are going to write an explanation for the alien. Ask the children to suggest words and phrases which could be used to begin their sentences, using the class list from the previous day. Show the children an enlarged copy of the writing frame on Copymaster 36. Use the shared writing process to model the first part of writing an explanation.

Group and independent work
Ask the children to write an explanation in answer to the question 'Why do humans wear clothes?'. Use Copymaster 36 as a structure. Encourage the children to add some to the key features of explanations discussed in Lesson two.

Differentiation
Low Attainers – Ask them to choose two reasons from the class brainstorm to copy and illustrate.
High Attainers – Ask this group to use the frame on Copymaster 36 as a basic structure, extending their work by adding their own sentences with appropriate beginnings.

Whole class
Ask some children to present their work. Focus on children who have used other key features of explanations in their work.

Lesson 4
Whole class

Use an enlarged copy of a life-cycle for shared reading. Read the explanation with the children. Ask the children if anyone can identify different ways in which this type of explanation is presented. Make a class list of any key features, *e.g. the use of boxes, arrows and numbers etc.* Show the children an enlarged photocopy of Copymaster 37 which has been cut into sections. Read each section with the children and ask them to put the sentences in the correct order. Ask the children to tell you ways in which you would make the explanation easier to read and follow, thinking about the examples they have looked at so far, *e.g. adding pictures, boxes, arrows and a title.* Begin to model the process of presenting the text as an explanation using the children's ideas.

Group and independent work
Ask the children to present the life-cycle of a butterfly using the key features of explanations discussed so far. You may want to give some children copies of Copymaster 37 to use for this text.

Differentiation
Low Attainers – Order, cut and stick their own copy of Copymaster 37 and add diagrams and any other key features to their work. Children may need some adult support to read the text.
High Attainers – Allow this group to write their own text to go with their diagrams, based on the text in Copymaster 37.

Whole class
Ask the children to swap their explanation with a partner. Ask the children if they can read and follow their partner's explanation. Encourage some children to feed back on effective features of presentation which have been used by their partner.

Lesson 5
Whole class

Begin by recapping on the explanations which have been read so far this week. Ask the children to tell you the key features of explanations which have been used in all these texts. Present the children with a selection of questions which they could answer in the form of an explanation, *e.g. Why do children have to go to school? What is the life-cycle of a frog? Why do people like to keep pets? Why do we need to eat healthy food?* Read each of the questions with the children and ask them to brainstorm three or four answers to each of the questions whilst the teacher records their answers. Ask the children to suggest appropriate ways of presenting each explanation. Remind the children of the class list of key features.

Group and independent work
Put the children into pairs. Give each pair a large sheet of paper and ask them to choose one of the questions to answer and present as an explanation. Remind the children to use the key features of presentation which are appropriate to their explanation.

Differentiation
Low Attainers – This group can choose one of the questions and produce a group explanation with the support of an adult.
High Attainers – The children can work in mixed ability pairs for this activity.

Whole class
Choose pairs of children to present their explanations to the rest of the class. Ask the children to evaluate each explanation, selecting key features of presentation which have been used effectively.

Theme 10 Dictionaries and other alphabetically ordered texts

Objectives

Text level
• 16 To use dictionaries to locate words by using initial letter;
• 17 To know that dictionaries give definitions and explanations, discuss what definitions are, explore some simple definitions in dictionaries;
• 18 To use other alphabetically ordered books and discuss how they are used.

Resources

A selection of different styles of dictionary. A range of other alphabetically ordered texts, e.g. phone book, Yellow Pages, catalogues, registers etc.
Class dictionaries, at least one copy per pair of children. Copymaster 38, Copymaster 39, a phone book, Yellow Pages. Homework 20.

Resource preparation

• Write each letter of the alphabet onto A5 sized card or paper for the children to order. One A3 sized copy of Copymaster 38 for every child.
• A selection of unknown words with invented definitions for a 'Call my bluff' style game (see Lesson 3).
• Photocopy of class name list.
• Use a local Yellow Pages, photocopy restaurant adverts and stick them at random onto an A4 sheet.

Assessment

At the end of this theme is the pupil able to:
• locate words in a dictionary using the initial letter;
• read and understand a simple definition in a dictionary;
• use a range of other alphabetically ordered texts?

Lesson 1

Whole class

Begin this week by giving each child a random letter from the alphabet. Tell the children holding the cards that you would like them to get themselves into alphabetical order without talking to each other. Check that they are in the correct order and together recite the alphabet. Leave the cards in alphabetical order and discuss the location of individual letters with the children. Do they come at the beginning, middle or end of the alphabet? Turn the alphabet cards over and ask the children to go and stand where they predict some letters of the alphabet are located. Reinforce the approximate location of various letters in the alphabet (beginning, middle or end). Introduce the children to the dictionary. Ask some children to locate various letters in the dictionary using their knowledge of alphabetical order.

Group and independent work
Give the children an enlarged copy of Copymaster 38.

Ask the children to use their knowledge of alphabetical order to put one letter into each box. When they have finished, ask the children to write the names of their favourite thing which begin with each letter into the correct box, e.g. a = apple, b = banana, c = cat.

Differentiation
Low Attainers – Use the alphabet cards to put the alphabet into their grid. This group can record their favourite things pictorially.
High Attainers – Ask children to select an adjective which describes themselves to go into each box, e.g. a – adorable, b – brave.

Whole class
Make sure the alphabet cards on the floor are turned over. Put the children into pairs. Ask one child to select a word from their grid. Their partner can go and stand by the card which they think corresponds to the initial letter in their partner's word.

Lesson 2

Whole class

Show a dictionary to the class and revise its format and uses. Remind the children of alphabetical order and the location of initial sounds in the dictionary. Remind the children that a dictionary contains words and their meanings. Introduce and discuss the term 'definition'. Using an enlarged version of Copymaster 39, explore the format of a definition with the children. Focus on the use of shortened sentences rather than full descriptive sentences. Put the children into pairs and give each pair a whiteboard. Ask the children to define a sample word using one sentence only, e.g. a chair, a dog. Ask the children to show their definitions to the class. Choose a good example to write on the board. Now ask the children if they can shorten the definition on the board to contain only four words. Ask the children to show their definitions. Explain to the children that people who

write definitions have to use as few words as possible whilst still keeping overall sense.

Whole class and independent work
Give the children a range of simple words and ask them to write their own definitions. Children may work in pairs for this task.

Differentiation
Low Attainers – Choose one or two words for this group to define. They could produce a group definition with adult support.
High Attainers – This group could be given more complex words to define. Ask them to check with a friend when they have finished to see if they could have used fewer words for their definition.

Whole class
Ask some children to read out their definitions to the class. Can the rest of the class guess the word being defined?

Lesson 3

Whole class

Ask the children to write the name of a food which they like to eat on a whiteboard. Tell the children that you would like them to get themselves into alphabetical order using the initial letter from their food. If any of the foods begin with the same letter, discuss the use of the second letter when ordering words alphabetically. Recap on the term definition and as a class generate a definition for one of the foods which a child has chosen. Tell the children that you are going to play a game where they have to select the correct definition for a word. Prepare two or three words that the children will not have come across. Invent two definitions for each word you have chosen. For each word, read the real definition to the children and the two definitions you have invented. Ask the class to vote for the definition that they think is correct.

Group and independent work

Give pairs, or groups of three children, a word or definition which is unfamiliar and the correct meaning of that word. Ask the children to invent two definitions which are false, to try to catch out the rest of the class. Remind the children of the language style used when writing a definition. This activity can be completed in mixed ability pairs or groups.

Differentiation

Low Attainers – The children can match correct definitions to objects or animals, e.g. *fish – a creature that swims in the sea.*

Whole class

Children read out their word and the three definitions. Ask the rest of the class to identify the correct meaning. Draw attention to definitions written in the appropriate form.

Lesson 4

Whole class

Ask children to think of other alphabetically ordered texts. Make a list. Show the children a phone book. Discuss how to use a phone book, revising alphabetical order. Explain the use of second and third letter to order names alphabetically, using some examples from the phone book. Model locating some of the children's names in the class. Ask if their names would come at the beginning, middle or end of the book. Model for the children how to set out a name and address from the phone book. Select five children from the class and ask them to tell the class their surnames. Ask the children if they can organise themselves into the order in which their names would appear in the phone book.

Group and independent work

Give the children a class name list. Ask them to write out the list in the style and order in which the names would appear in the phone book. A shortened list may be appropriate for some children.

Differentiation

Low Attainers – Cut up a class list and sort names alphabetically.

Whole class

Ask the class to order themselves alphabetically according to their surnames.

Lesson 5

Whole class

Show the children a copy of the Yellow Pages. Ask the children if they know what it is and how it is used. Compare the layout of the phone book used in Lesson 4 and the Yellow Pages. Tell the children that you want to go out for a meal on Saturday. Can anyone demonstrate how to use the Yellow Pages to find a restaurant? Model this process with the children. Invent the names of several restaurants and write them onto card. Give the cards to children and ask them to order themselves alphabetically. Make a photocopiable sheet by copying restaurant adverts from the Yellow Pages and sticking them onto a sheet of A4 paper. Tell the children that this particular page has become muddled and you need their help to put it in order.

Group and independent work

Give pairs of children a copy of the 'restaurant' Yellow Pages sheet. Ask children to cut out the adverts and stick them in alphabetical order. Tell the children to look out for adverts which begin with the same initial letter. It is a good idea to tell the children to number the adverts before they start to cut them out.

Differentiation

Low Attainers – Select adverts for this group to put in alphabetical order by initial letter only. This group may need to see the alphabet in order to help them with this task.
High Attainers – Give this group a couple of adverts only. Ask them to invent their own restaurant adverts in the same style. Put the adverts in alphabetical order.

Whole class

Cut out the adverts from the Yellow Pages 'restaurant' sheet and give them to children in the class. Ask these children to put themselves in alphabetical order. Focus on inaccuracies, particularly where two names begin with the same letter. Ask the children to tell you what they have found out about dictionaries and other alphabetically ordered texts this week. Make a list on a board.

Theme 1) Different stories by the same author (week 1)

This unit of work is a three week programme which enables the children to look at various aspects of Martin Waddell stories leading into the comparison of his books. This will then allow the children to comment on Martin Waddell as an author.

Objectives
Text level
- 4 To compare books by the same author: settings, characters, themes, and to evaluate, giving reasons;
- 5 To read about authors from information on book covers and to become aware of authorship and publication;
- 12 To write simple evaluations of books read and discussed giving reasons.

Resources
A selection of texts by Martin Waddell, which includes three big books to be used as focus texts over the three weeks. It is useful to select three texts with some similar elements, such as 'Farmer Duck', 'Owl Babies', 'Can't you sleep little bear?' or 'Pig in the pond', which all have animals as main characters.
Copymasters 40 and 41. Homework 21.

Resource preparation
It is useful to have some information about Martin Waddell as an author. There is information about him on the internet if you search 'Martin Waddell', or if you phone the publishers, 'Walker Books', they will send you an author information pack.
Collect Martin Waddell books for a class display.

Assessment
At the end of this theme is the pupil able to:
- recognise Martin Waddell as a significant children's author;
- identify the setting, characters and themes within a text which they have read;
- identify similarities and differences between texts written by the same author;
- state their opinion on given texts and give reasons?

Lesson 1
Whole class

Begin this unit by asking the children if they know what an author is. Do they know the names of any famous authors? Initiate a class brainstorm recording the names of the authors which the children know. Pick out any significant children's author and ask the children what type of book that particular author writes, *e.g. adventure stories, humorous stories, spooky tales.* Explain to the children that most authors prefer writing a certain style of text. Introduce the children to the term 'publisher' and explain to the children that all authors have a publisher who checks, prints and sells the books for them. Locate the name of a publisher on a variety of books in the classroom. Do the children know the names of any other book publishers?

Group and independent work
Select a range of books by various authors and put them on the tables. Ask the children to look at as many books as they can and record the title, author's name and the publisher of the book. Challenge the children to find books which have been published by the same company or written by the same author. Include some books by Martin Waddell.

Differentiation
Low Attainers – This can be a verbal activity, discussing the title, author and publisher without recording their work. An adult can record their findings if appropriate.
High Attainers – Ask the children to comment on the style of each book and look for trends. Do books written by the same author have a similar style of text?

Whole class
The teacher can record the class findings looking for books published by the same company. How many different companies did we find?
Define the terms 'author' and 'publisher' together.

Lesson 2
Whole class

Recap on the terms 'author' and 'publisher'. Ask the children if anyone found any books by Martin Waddell in the previous lesson. Does anyone know the names of any of his other books? Explain to the children that over the next few weeks you are going to read some books by Martin Waddell and think about whether they would recommend any of his books to a friend to read. Read the first few pages of the first text with the children. It doesn't matter in which order you read them. Ask the children to tell you where the story takes place. Does anyone know the proper name for this? Revise the term 'setting' and ask the children why they think Martin Waddell has chosen that particular setting for the story you are reading. Is there more than one setting for the story? Ask the children to think of adjectives which they could use to describe the settings. This can be discussed in pairs using the 'time out' strategy.

Group and independent work
Ask the children to define the word 'setting' and brainstorm adjectives they would use to describe the setting of the first Martin Waddell book. When they have finished, they can illustrate their work.

Differentiation
Low Attainers – Record work pictorially. Children can either describe the setting to a friend or record descriptive words with adult support if appropriate.
High Attainers – Encourage children to write in sentences. Ask them to explain why they think Martin Waddell chose that particular setting for his story.

Whole class
Ask the children to brainstorm settings of other stories they know. Do any authors use similar settings?

48

Lesson 3

Whole class

Begin by reading the whole text with the children. Ask the children to identify the characters in the story and make a list. Can the children think of adjectives to describe each character, thinking about appearance and personality? Encourage the children to use the text to justify their opinions. Ask the children if anyone would like to try to pretend to be one of the characters from the story, using mime only. Encourage the use of body language and facial expressions (the teacher could model this for the children initially). See if the rest of the class can guess which character you or the children are pretending to be.

Group and independent work
Ask the children to select one of the main characters in the story and draw him/her/it in the centre of the page. Can they produce a profile of their chosen character with their description on one side and their personality on the other? You can use Copymaster 40 for this activity.

Differentiation
Low Attainers – This activity can be recorded pictorially with descriptive words around the outside if appropriate.
High Attainers – Ask the children to give examples from the text to justify their comments.

Whole class
Ask some children to read their descriptions without showing the class their work. Can the rest of the class guess the character they are describing?

Lesson 4

Whole class

Recap the main events of the text. Introduce the children to the term 'theme'. What do you think Martin Waddell is trying to tell people through his book? Is he trying to make them feel better about something, teach them a lesson, make them laugh? Explain to the children that this is the theme of the book. Tell the children that you are going to write a simple review of the book, thinking about the settings, characters and themes. Write a simple frame on the board using these three headings. Use the children's ideas to model writing a sentence for each of the headings. Encourage the children to think about their own opinions and to explain why they think as they do, *e.g. I think the farmer is lazy because in the story he doesn't do any work (Farmer Duck).* Keep this writing frame for the following day.

Group and independent work
Using the three headings, ask the children to continue a review of the text, focusing on giving reasons for their opinions.

Differentiation
Low Attainers – This activity can be completed orally. Alternatively the children can write a sentence giving their opinions of the text and a reason for this, with adult support or the use of flash cards as prompts.
High Attainers – Ask children to give an opinion on what age group Martin Waddell wrote this particular story for and why. Encourage the use of extended sentences using connectives.

Whole class
Ask the children to share their opinions with the rest of the class. Have they given reasons for their opinions?

Lesson 5

Whole class

Ask the children if they know what you would find on the back of a text. Read the blurb with the children. Ask the children if they think it tells you the whole story. Why not? What else can be found on the back apart from the outline of the story? Why do you think the publishers include newspaper reviews on the back of the stories? Ask the children to imagine that they work for a newspaper and are going to write a review in the style of a newspaper. Use the 'time out' strategy to allow the children to work in pairs to invent a one line, newspaper style review to go on the back of the book. Allow the children to present their ideas to the class.

Group and independent work
In mixed ability pairs children can complete their own blurb for the text you are reading. This should include a brief outline of the story along with one or two newspaper reviews. The children will enjoy inventing their own names for newspapers.

Differentiation
Low Attainers – The children can be paired with a more able child for this activity.
High Attainers – Encourage the children to think carefully about the style of a newspaper review when making word choices for this.

Whole class
Ask the children to come to the front and present their blurbs in pairs in the style of a newspaper reporter. Focus on the choice of descriptive language made by the children.
Discuss and summarise unit.

Theme 2) Different stories by the same author (week 2)

Objectives

Text level

- 4 To compare books by the same author: settings, characters, themes, and to evaluate, giving reasons;
- 5 To read about authors from information on book covers and to become aware of authorship and publication;
- 12 To write simple evaluations of books read and discussed giving reasons.

Resources

The second big book by Martin Waddell.

A range of texts written by Martin Waddell. Copymasters 41 and 42. Homework 22.

Assessment

At the end of this theme is the pupil able to:
- recognise Martin Waddell as a significant children's author;
- identify the setting, characters and themes within a text which they have read;
- identify similarities and differences between texts written by the same author;
- state their opinion on given texts and give reasons?

Lesson 1

Whole class

Begin this second week by reminding the children of the author Martin Waddell. Ask the children if they can remember the names of any texts which he has written. Explain to the children that you will be looking in detail at another Martin Waddell text this week and thinking about how this text compares with the book they read last week. Read the first few pages of the book together. Can the children remember what the term setting means? Ask the children to identify the setting in this particular story. Put the children into pairs and give each pair a whiteboard. Ask the children to write two adjectives they could use to describe the setting of the book. Make a class list of adjectives and compare these to the description of settings from week 1. Ask the children to identify similarities and differences between the settings.

Group and independent work

Describe and compare the settings of the two Martin Waddell texts using Copymaster 41.

Differentiation

Low Attainers – This activity can be completed pictorially. The children can then brainstorm words to accompany their picture with adult support if appropriate.

High Attainers – Encourage the children to think about why Martin Waddell chose these settings and complete the extension activity on Copymaster 41.

Lesson 2

Whole class

Read the whole text with the class and discuss the story. Recap on the term 'characters'. Make a class list of the characters which appear in this story. Choose a main character from the story and tell the children that together you are going to try to find out more about that particular character. Ask the class if anyone would like to come out to the front and pretend to be that character whilst the other children ask them questions. If there are no volunteers, the teacher may have to take on this role. Tell that child to think about the behaviour of that particular character in the story. When the class counts to five that child will no longer be themselves but will be the character in the story. Give a few children a question to ask the child pretending to be the character or the children may be able to think of their own questions if they have done this activity before. These questions should enable the children to explore the reasons for a character's actions in the story. Allow the children to ask their questions to the character, supporting the child being questioned where appropriate. Make sure you count down again as a class, in order to bring the volunteer out of their role. Discuss and list the things you have found out about that particular character.

Group and independent work

Ask the children to select a character from the story. Put the children into pairs and give each pair the list of questions from the whole class session. The children can then interview each other in turn, with each child taking on the role of their chosen character.

Differentiation

Low Attainers – This activity can be completed in mixed ability pairs. Try to pair quiet children with more confident peers.

High Attainers – Encourage children to think of their own questions.

Whole class

Give a brief description of each character using the information obtained from the class activity.

Lesson 3
Whole class

Sit the children in a circle and re-tell the story of this week's chosen text by asking the children to give a sentence each. Recap on the term 'theme'. Ask the children to consider the theme of this book. What message does Martin Waddell want to give to his readers through the book? Is he trying to help us to understand something? Do the children know any other stories with a similar theme? Think about the theme of the previous week's text. Are there any similarities or differences between the two themes?

Use shared writing to complete a written explanation of the theme of the book with the children. Focus on the messages Martin Waddell is aiming to give through his stories related to the age of his audience. For example, the theme of 'Can't you sleep little bear?' is fear of the dark. This attempts to reassure young children who have been afraid of the dark themselves.

Group and independent work
Complete a written explanation of the themes from both of the texts read so far using the shared writing generated in whole class work as a model. Add a sentence at the end which comments on any similarities between the two texts.

Differentiation
Low Attainers – Sequence the story pictorially using four boxes. Encourage the children to give a verbal report on the theme of each text.
High Attainers – Add a further sentence to the work which explains why they think Martin Waddell has chosen these particular themes to write about.

Whole class
Discuss the reasons why Martin Waddell might have chosen these themes for his stories. Ask the children to think about the age of child he is writing for.

Lesson 4
Whole class

Tell the children that today you are going to compare the two books which you have read so far and think about any similarities and differences between them. Remind the children of the writing frame which was used in week 1, Lesson 4. Ask the children to think about categories which can now be added to this frame when reviewing the text. What other aspects of the book might a future reader want to know about, e.g. illustrations, humour, cost of book, plot? Try to add two or three categories to your class writing frame, including a sentence at the end which looks at similarities and differences between the two texts. Save any comments on personal opinions for the following day.

Group and independent work
Complete a review of this week's text using the writing frame constructed during the whole class session. Ensure that the children make comparisons between both texts highlighting similarities and differences.

Differentiation
Low Attainers – Give a verbal review of each text thinking about settings, plot and characters. This can be recorded to be fed back at the end of the session.
High Attainers – Encourage children to support their comments with examples from the text.

Whole class
Ask the children to feed back on their reviews. Focus particularly on similarities between this text and other books by Martin Waddell.

Lesson 5
Whole class

Ask the children to consider which has been their favourite text so far. What are their reasons? Sit them in a circle and ask each child in turn to select their favourite text and give one reason for their choice. Have the two texts available and encourage the children to refer to the text when they are selecting their reasons. Tell the children that they are going to give a personal review of their favourite Martin Waddell book so far. Model part of this process for them using an enlarged version of Copymaster 42.

Group and independent work
Complete a review of their favourite Martin Waddell book so far using Copymaster 42.

Differentiation
Low Attainers – Draw the front cover of their favourite Martin Waddell text. Complete a sentence giving a reason for their choice. This can be completed with support if appropriate.
High Attainers – Encourage children to use Copymaster 42 as a frame only and complete and work on paper or in their books. This will allow them to develop the content of their work.

Whole class
Hold a class vote on their favourite text so far. Consider the qualities which make this text particularly appealing to their age range.

Theme 3) Different stories by the same author (week 3)

Objectives
Text level
- 4 To compare books by the same author: settings, characters, themes, and to evaluate, giving reasons;
- 5 To read about authors from information on book covers and to become aware of authorship and publication;
- 12 To write simple evaluations of books read and discussed giving reasons?

Resources
A collection of books written by Martin Waddell.
The third big book text written by Martin Waddell.

Copymaster 43, Copymaster 44. Homework 23.

Assessment
At the end of this theme is the pupil able to:
- recognise Martin Waddell as a significant children's author;
- identify the setting, characters and themes within a text which they have read;
- identify similarities and differences between texts written by the same author;
- state their opinion on given texts and give reasons?

Lesson 1
Whole class

Explain to the children that this is the last week you will be looking at Martin Waddell texts. Recap on the stories you have looked at so far, asking the children to give a brief outline of each book. Show the children the last big book by Martin Waddell. Ask the children if they can predict the setting of the text from looking at the front cover. Have we seen this setting in any other Martin Waddell books? Read the first few pages of the text with the children and discuss whether their predictions were correct. Choose one or two other texts by Martin Waddell from the class collection. Can the children establish the setting of each text without reading the book? Discuss the similarities and differences between the settings in Martin Waddell books.

Group and independent work
Put a selection of books by Martin Waddell on each table. Ask the children to record the title and setting of each. When they have completed this, ask them to list any similarities and differences between the settings in Martin Waddell stories.

Differentiation
Low Attainers – Record the title of each text and a picture of each setting. Children can add words or sentences to their work with adult support if appropriate.
High Attainers – Ask children to consider the atmosphere that Martin Waddell is trying to create through his use of settings.

Whole class
Discuss the similarities and differences between the settings in books. Ask the children to make generalisations about the settings in Martin Waddell's texts, *e.g. He likes to set some of his stories on farms.*

Lesson 2
Whole class

Begin by reading the whole of the third Martin Waddell text with the children. Ask the children to identify the characters in the new text and make a list. Discuss briefly the attributes of each character. Ask the children to consider whether any of the characters remind them of characters from other Martin Waddell stories. Can they notice any similarities and differences? *e.g. Often the characters are animals, sometimes the characters are afraid of something.* Ask the children to select two characters from Martin Waddell stories who are similar in some way. Ask each child to state their chosen characters and give an example of something which is similar about them. Use one child's example to model how to record this using an enlarged version of Copymaster 43.

Group and independent work
Give each child a copy of Copymaster 43. Ask them to use this structure to compare the two characters they chose in the whole class session.

Differentiation
Low Attainers – Draw two pictures of similar characters, brainstorming adjectives around the edge. Consider similarities and differences orally.
High Attainers – Encourage children to think carefully about their choice of adjectives when describing characters.

Whole class
Discuss similarities between Martin Waddell characters. Can children make any generalisations about Martin Waddell's characters? *e.g. He often writes about animals.*

Lesson 3

Whole class

Show the children the writing frame which was used in weeks 1 and 2. Tell them that you are going to add to this frame today and use it to compare the three Martin Waddell texts which they have read over the past three weeks. Ask the children to try to think of an extra category which could be added to the frame which compares all three Martin Waddell books. Tell them that you would like to know their opinion of Martin Waddell texts by asking them to say whether they would read another book written by him. Encourage the children to give reasons for their answer. Put the children into pairs and use the 'time out' strategy to discuss their opinion with a partner. Tell the children to listen carefully to their partner as they may be asked to tell the class their partner's answer. Ask some children to tell you whether their partner would read another text by Martin Waddell and the reasons they gave for their answers. Add a sentence to the class writing frame which says 'I would/would not read another book by Martin Waddell because . . . '.

Group and independent work

Give each child a sheet of A3 size paper folded into three sections. Ask the children to write the name of each book at the top of the folded boxes. Ask the children to compare the three books using the structure of the class writing frame. The headings for the frame can be written down the side of the sheet of paper. Ask the children to give each book a score out of ten.

Differentiation

Low Attainers – Complete a differentiated frame with given sentence starters, *e.g. 'My favourite character is . . .', 'My favourite book was . . .', 'I would/would not read another Martin Waddell book'.*
High Attainers – Encourage children to add further categories to their writing frame related to the comparison of all three books.

Whole class

Ask the children to give their scores for each book and use this information to vote for a class favourite. Consider the reasons why that particular text was the most popular.

Lesson 4

Whole class

Start by telling the children that you need their help with a problem. Explain that one of the Reception (or Year 1) teachers would like to read some Martin Waddell books to his/her children but would like to know a little bit more about him and his stories. A letter to the children from that particular teacher could be used as a stimulus for this activity. Discuss with the children whether Martin Waddell's stories would be suitable for younger children. How would they describe him as an author to this teacher? What common things have we found in his stories? As a class, devise a writing frame for the children to use for their reply during independent working time or use Copymaster 44. Ideas which could be included are:
'I would/would not recommend Martin Waddell to you.'

'The characters in his stories are . . .'
'The themes he uses are . . .'
'I think you would particularly enjoy . . . because . . .'

Group and independent work

Ask the children to reply to the teacher's letter using the frame which was constructed during the whole class session. Encourage them to give reasons for their answers.

Differentiation

Low Attainers – Children can either recommend one text giving a reason to support their answer or discuss their reply with an adult and record this onto a tape recorder.
High Attainers – Encourage children to refer to the texts to give examples to illustrate their answers.

Whole class

Ask some children to read their recommendations. Which book was the class favourite?

Lesson 5

Whole class

Ask the children to think about the sheet they were given to complete for homework during the previous week (the children were asked to list books they had read which were written by the same author). Ask them if anyone in the class has got a favourite author. Encourage any volunteers to give some examples of that particular author's books and reasons as to why they like them. Explain that they are going to make a class book called 'Our favourite authors'. List on the board the authors that some of the children are going to write about. There may be children who or are not sure of one particular author. Remind them of any authors which you have read together. Some of these children may want to write about traditional tales instead. Explain to the children that they are going to try to persuade the rest of the class to read some books by their chosen author. Write some prompt questions on

the board to help the children with this, *e.g. What is the author's name?, What types of books does that author write?*

Group and independent work

Ask children to write a review of their favourite author using prompt questions as a guide. Some children may require a writing frame to complete this task.

Differentiation

Low Attainers – Draw a picture of their favourite traditional tale, adding a sentence explaining why they like that particular story.
High Attainers – Complete the task using the prompt questions only. Encourage the children to think about descriptive words and phrases which will persuade their friends to read books by their chosen author.

Whole class

Ask some children to read their author reviews. Ask the rest of the class if the children's reviews have made them want to read books by other authors?

Theme 4) Texts with language play: riddles

Objectives

Text level

- 6 To read and collect examples of riddles;
- 11 To use riddles as a structure for children to write their own by adaptation, selecting words with care.

Sentence level

- 6 To turn statements into questions; learning a range of 'wh' words typically used to open questions: what, where, when, who, and to add question marks.

Resources

'Guess what I am' by Anni Axworthy.

Poetry books containing riddles. Riddles typed onto card.
Sugar paper book for completed riddles. Picture of animal.
Copymasters 45 and 46. Homework 24.

Assessment

At the end of this theme is the pupil able to:
- identify and read riddles with appropriate expression;
- write their own riddles using a given structure;
- compose their own questions?

Lesson 1

Whole class

Introduce the text 'Guess what I am' and read the first double page spread with the class. Ask the children what sort of text they think it is. Draw attention to the question and the following facts that give clues. Then turn the page over for the answer. Write the word 'riddle' on the board. Tell the children that they have just read a riddle and ask them to think about what a riddle could be as they read the rest of the book. Continue reading the book together. Draw out features of riddles, i.e. questions and statements which form a puzzle and need to be solved by the listener or reader. Tell the children that sometimes the writer does not answer the riddle for the reader: they have to do it for themselves. Ask the children if they know any riddles. They may offer jokes they know. Tell the children that during the week they are going to write their own riddle about an animal or bird.

Group and independent work

Ask children to find and read riddles either from selected books or riddles typed onto card. Use riddles on Copymasters 45 and 46. Encourage children to work in pairs and read their chosen riddle to a partner who has to guess the answer.

Differentiation

Low Attainers – Re-read 'Guess what I am' with adult help.
High Attainers – After reading a selection of riddles, children write their own definition of a riddle.

Whole class

Ask some children to read out their riddle and the rest of the class have to guess the answer. Tell the children that before the next lesson they must decide which animal or bird they want to write a riddle about and ask them to find out how to spell correctly the name of their chosen animal or bird.

Lesson 2

Whole class

Show the children a picture of your chosen animal. Write the name of the animal at the top of a board or a large piece of paper. Tell the children that before you start to write your riddle you need to think of some questions about the animal. Give the children 'time out' in pairs to think of questions to ask about your animal. Take some examples and write them onto the board, *e.g. What do elephants eat? Why do elephants have long trunks?* Choose four questions to write on the board. Number the questions. Discuss the use of question marks. Look at the first word of each question. Draw attention to the use of 'why', 'what', 'when'.

zGroup and independent work

Ask children to write four questions in relation to their chosen animal or bird ensuring they:
- head their work with the animal's or bird's name;
- number each question;
- begin each question with 'why', 'what', or 'when';
- put a question mark at the end of each question.

Differentiation

Low Attainers – Think of questions orally. Encourage children to try to compose questions onto a whiteboard.
High Attainers – Encourage children to think of interesting questions.

Whole class

Read questions from the high attainers group. Answer the questions orally.

Lesson 3

Whole class

Return to the questions about your chosen animal written with the class in Lesson 2. Read the questions with the children. Ask the children to help you to answer the questions. Write the answers on another sheet of paper, *e.g. Elephants eat leaves*. Read the questions and answers together making sure they make sense. Check for full stops and capital letters.

Ask children to sit in pairs and read their questions to a partner who must try to answer the questions.

Group and independent work

Ask children to write their own questions. You may need to have some reference books available.

Differentiation

Low Attainers – Scribe for children and encourage them to re-read their work.

High Attainers – Encourage children to read their questions and answers to each other when complete and discuss the answers.

Whole class

Ask children to sit with a partner. Model reading questions written by children and ask that child to read their answers aloud. Tell pairs to read questions and answers together. Support low attainers or organise mixed ability pairings.

Lesson 4

Whole class

Tell the children they are going to use work from Lesson 3 to start writing their riddles. Write 'Who am I?' on the board, leaving out the question mark. Ask the children what is missing. Look at the answers written in whole class work during Lesson 3. Read through the first answer together. Return briefly to 'Guess what I am' and look at how the riddles are structured, *e.g. lines begin with 'I am …', 'I …' or 'my …'*. Ask children how they could make this into the first line of a riddle. Work through the four answers composing a riddle. Ask children how they could complete the riddle by giving the answer, i.e. I am a … Read the riddle together.

Group and independent work

Children use answers written in Lesson 3 and compose their own riddles using whole class work as a model.

Differentiation

Low Attainers – Compose riddles orally or encourage children to compose their own onto a whiteboard.

High Attainers – Ask the children to think carefully about their choice of words, so that the reader has to think hard about what the animal or bird could be.

Whole class

Ask the children who would like to read their riddles. Tell them not to give the answers. The rest of the class have to guess the animal or bird.

Lesson 5

Whole class

Enlarge or write out a couple of the children's riddles. Ask permission first. Read the riddles together. Discuss the riddles in relation to:
• choice of words;
• use of punctuation;
• spelling.

Group and independent work

Encourage children to reread their own work and improve before copying and illustrating or word processing. Children can stick their completed riddle into a book. This can then be shared with younger children who have to try to solve the riddles.

Whole class

Ask children who would like to read their riddles. (Choose different children from those who read in Lesson 4.) Tell the rest of the class to guess the animal or bird.

Theme 5) Texts with language play – humorous verse

Objectives

Text level

- 8 To discuss meanings of words and phrases that create humour;
- 11 To use humorous verse as a structure for children to write their own adaptations.

Sentence level

- 1 To read text aloud with intonation and expression appropriate to the grammar and punctuation.

Word level

- 10 To use synonyms and other alternative words/ phrases that express same or similar meanings.

Resources

A selection of texts containing humorous verses e.g.

'Nonsense! Poems' chosen by Richard Brown and Kate Ruttle, CUP (1996).
'Walking the Bridge of Your Nose, Word Play, Rhymes, Poems' selected by Michael Rosen, Kingfisher (1997).
'Silly Verse for Kids' Spike Milligan, Puffin 1968.
Copies of traditional nursery rhymes.
Copies of Nonsense Nursery Rhymes from 'Nonsense Nursery Rhymes' by Richard Edwards and Chris Fisher.
Copymasters 47, 48, 49 amd 50. Homework 25.

Assessment

At the end of this theme is the pupil able to:

- read chosen poems confidently, with intonation and expression;
- discuss features of humorous poetry;
- write adaptations of chosen poems?

Lesson 1

Whole class

Draw the children's attention to the display of poetry books. Choose two or three examples and look at the front covers of the books. Ask the children what sort of poems they think the books contain. Read the titles of the books and discuss the illustrations. Ask the children how they think the authors are trying to show humour. Highlight collections of poems. Discuss the terms 'compiled', 'selected', 'chosen'.
Read 'On the Ning Nang Nong' by Spike Milligan (Copymaster 47).
Re-read with the children. Ask the children what they think the poem is about. Ask them if they think it is funny, and why. Discuss the humour and the use of nonsense words.

Group and independent work

Give groups appropriate selections of humorous poems. Ask children to look through the books and choose their favorite poem. Tell the children to read their chosen poem to a partner and prepare to read to the whole class.

Differentiation

Low Attainers – Prepare a group reading of one poem with adult support.
High Attainers – Encourage children to prepare a poem using appropriate rhythm and expression.

Whole class

Some children present their chosen poems. Children vote on their favourite poem.

Lesson 2

Whole class

Return to 'On the Ning Nang Nong' with the following words covered: cows, monkeys, trees, teapots, mice.
Read the poem with the children and clap the missing words using an appropriate number of syllables.
Discuss the need for one or two syllable words to fill in the spaces.
Ask the children to provide substitute words. Discuss the choice and select words to fill the spaces.
Read the poem again with the newly chosen words. Discuss the two versions. Which one do the children prefer and why?

Group and independent work

- Give children copies of 'On the Ning Nang Nong' (Copymaster 47) with words omitted. Ask children to substitute alternative words to those composed in the whole class activity.
- Children return to their chosen poem from Lesson 1, copy and illustrate for class anthology.

Differentiation

High Attainers – Using 'On the Ning Nang Nong', delete a range of rhyming words and ask children to substitute their own rhyming pattern.

Whole class

Read poems with substitute words. Discuss word choices. Are they funny? why?

Lesson 3

Whole class

Put an enlarged copy of Copymaster 48 on the board. Ask children to try to read the traditional nursery rhyme to themselves. Support low attainers. Choose one child to read the rhyme to the rest of the class. Read the rhyme with the whole class. Put an enlarged copy of Copymaster 49 on the board (a nonsense nursery rhyme). Give children time to read the rhyme individually and then read with the whole class. Compare the two versions. Look carefully at the rhyme. Find which lines are the same in both rhymes.

Group and independent work
- Ask children to work in pairs and read both copies of their rhyme to their partner. Ask the children to write down words and phrases that they think make the rhyme humorous.
- Continue preparation of class anthology.

Whole class
Discuss words and phrases from a selection of rhymes that create humour.

Lesson 4

Whole class

Read with the class a selection of tongue twisters, e.g. from Silly Patters in 'Walking the Bridge of Your Nose' by Michael Rosen (examples appear on Copymaster 50). Choose tongue twisters that make use of alliteration for effect. Discuss alliteration. Highlight any words with the same sound but different spelling, e.g. 'fly and a flea flew up a flue'.
Working together, compose an alliterative sentence.

Group and independent work
Using whiteboards and pens, children compose their own alliterative sentence, revising it until they are happy with their word choices. Encourage children to check spellings. Ask the children to write their sentence onto paper for inclusion in the class anthology.

Differentiation
High Attainers – Children can continue adding to their alliterative sentence to make a longer tongue twister.

Whole class
Sitting in a circle give all children an opportunity to share their alliterative sentences.

Lesson 5

Whole class

Write on the board two tongue twisters that children have brought from home. Re-read each line as you write. Read the whole tongue twister and then cover and encourage the class/groups/individuals to recite from memory. Ask the children why saying the tongue twister is difficult. Return to alliterative sentences from Lesson 4. Use several examples in the same way.

Group and independent work
Finish contributions to the class anthology:
- rewriting and illustrating favourite poem;
- preparing examples of adapted 'On the Ning Nang Nong' poems;
- completing alliterative sentences.

Whole class
Discuss with the children what they have done this week. Ask them to discuss with a partner what they liked best and why. Look at the class anthology. Choose one poem to read from it. Highlight the similarities between the children's anthology and published anthologies the class have read.

Theme 6) Extended stories (week 1)

The next 3 units of work will form a bridge between Year 2 and Year 3 literacy work and should be carried out towards the end of the summer term. Some children will already be reading longer stories themselves, whilst others will enjoy having longer stories read to them and will be able to share extracts and classroom discussion about texts. Many activities build on previous work carried out during the year.

Objectives

Text level
- 3 To notice the difference between spoken and written forms through re-telling known stories and to compare oral versions with the written text;
- 5 To read about authors from information on book covers;
- 7 To compare books by different authors on similar themes.

Sentence
- 2 To recognise the need for grammatical agreement, matching verbs to nouns/pronouns and using simple gender forms.

Resources
- Two stories on similar themes. For this work one is a collection of stories, the other one a story in chapters. Reference will be made to the following texts: 'Twig Thing' by Jan Mark and 'The Julian Stories' by Ann Cameron;
- Enlarged 'blurb' from the back of texts;
- Enlarged author details;
- Copymaster 51 Copymaster 52, Copymaster 53. Homework 26.

Assessment
At the end of this theme is the pupil able to:
- compare oral and written texts and understand the differences between them;
- find out information about authors by reading book covers;
- compare texts by different authors on a similar theme?

Lesson 1

Whole class

Tell the children that you are going to be looking at two longer books over the next 3 weeks and they are going to write a similar, longer story and read them to younger children at the end of term.
Look at the front covers of the two books. Read the titles. Ask the children what they think the books might be about. Ask the children to vote for the book they think may be best from looking at the front cover. Read the blurbs together. Have any of them changed their minds? Point out that one book is one long story and the other is six stories about the same character. Do they know which is which from the blurb and the title? Open the books and look at the contents pages. Ask the children why it is useful to divide longer books into sections or chapters. Fill in an enlarged a version of Copymaster 51 for the two books.

Group and independent work
Give children a selection of longer stories by a range of authors. Ask them to look at three books and put details onto Copymaster 51.

Differentiation
Low Attainers – Carry out this activity with a range of picture books.
High Attainers – Encourage children to read the beginning of the stories to increase their knowledge of the texts.

Whole class
Ask some children to recommend a book and justify their choice, making reference to Copymaster 51.

Lesson 2

Whole class

Photocopy and enlarge the author information from both books. Read with the children. Give pairs 'time out' to discuss the content of author information. Make a list of contents on the board. Ask children to highlight similarities and differences between the two authors. Tell the children that they are going to write author information about themselves. Ask for a volunteer who would like help with their author information. Ask the children how to start. Draw attention to the use of 'he' or 'she' rather than 'I'. Use one child as an example and write with the class the first two sentences, referring to the list of points.

Group and independent work
Children write their own author information, using the structure of the shared writing and including at least four points.

Differentiation
Low Attainers – Children compose their author information orally. An adult could write or children could be encouraged to write using the shared writing model to write their own details.

Whole class
Ask for volunteers to read their author information to the class. Comment on the way they are written, *e.g. praising grammatical agreement.*

Lesson 3

Whole class

Read 'The Pudding like a Night on the Sea' to the class from 'The Julian Stories'. Tell the children to listen carefully because you want them to re-tell the story afterwards. (Tape record the story as you are reading it.) Ask the children to sit in a circle. Start to re-tell the story simply, *e.g. 'Julian's father wanted to make something special for Julian's mother'*. Ask children to carry on the re-telling. Do not write the sequence but reiterate points after the re-telling.

Group and independent work

Ask children to use Copymaster 52 and fill in the first column. Most children should be able to do this independently as they will have had practice in planning stories during the year.

Differentiation

Low Attainers – Children listen to your taped reading again and discuss the story with an adult, filling in Copymaster 52 together.
High Attainers – Stress the need for note form to give story details.

Whole class

Use an enlarged copy of Copymaster 52. Ask children to refer to their work and fill in column 1 together. Model note form and brevity.

Lesson 4

Whole class

Read the first section of 'Twig Thing', 'Upstairs and Upstairs', to the children. Tell them to listen for the main points of the story. Discuss similarities and differences between this story and that read in Lesson 3. Fill in the second column of enlarged Copymaster 52 as far as you can. Discuss why you can't say what happened at the end. Ask the children to predict what might happen in the next chapter of the story. Take one idea and write on the board in note form.

Group and independent work

Ask children to work with a partner and think of three different ways of continuing the story. Give each pair a sheet of paper folded into three sections. Tell the children not to write the story.

Differentiation

Low Attainers – Ask the children to draw the next part of the story and write a caption.

Whole class

Ask pairs to feed back their ideas. Pick out the range of ideas and discuss the best way to continue.

Lesson 5

Whole class

Write the titles of the next three chapters of 'Twig Thing' on the board. Tell the children to listen to the rest of the story and that they need to be able to tell you three things that happened in each chapter. Did anyone agree with the author when thinking about what would happen next in Lesson 4? Note events from the story on a board at the end of each chapter. Complete Copymaster 52 together. Show the children Copymaster 53. Read through the sheet together and discuss one of the points. *e.g. I would/would not recommend this book to . . .*

Group and independent work

Ask the children to evaluate the story using Copymaster 53.

Differentiation

Low Attainers – Write a simplified evaluation, *e.g. I liked/ did not like the story because . . .*

Whole class

Ask children to sit in a circle and read their evaluation to their neighbour. Ask for a thumbs up or down quick evaluation of their partner's views about the book.

Theme 7) Extended stories (week 2)

Objectives

Text level
• 10 To write sustained stories using their knowledge of story elements: narrative, setting, characterisation, dialogue and the language of story.

Resources
'Twig Thing' by Jan Mark.
'The Julian stories' by Ann Cameron.

Enlarged and completed Copymaster 48 from week 1. Copymaster 54, Copymaster 55, Copymaster 56. Homework 27.

Assessment
At the end of this theme is the pupil able to:
• utilise their knowledge of story elements to create their own stories?

Lesson 1

Whole class

Read together Copymaster 54, the beginning of the Julian story 'Because of Figs'. Give children whiteboards and ask them to write:
• where they think the story is set;
• the name of the person who is telling the story.
Read Copymaster 55, from 'Twig Thing' by Jan Mark. Ask the children the same questions. Tell them to record their answers on the whiteboard. Lower attaining children may need support.
Look at enlarged and completed Copymaster 52 from week 1. How many of the points from this sheet are introduced in the first part of the stories? Discuss the introduction of the problem. Re-read Copymaster 54 and Copymaster 55. Is the problem introduced at the beginning of the stories?
Tell the children that they are going to start planning their stories, which they can model on either of the texts you have been using, i.e. write about something else that happens to Rosie and Ella in their new home or write about something else that happens to Julian.

Remind children that they must write as if they are Julian.
Brainstorm the sorts of things that could happen, *e.g. find something, lose something, break something, get lost, make something, have a visitor.*
Organise an audience for the work for the end of week 3, *e.g. a visit to a younger class to read the stories or a visit to the class from the Year 3 teacher.*

Group and independent work
Using children's copies of Copymaster 52 from week 1, ask the children to plan their stories using the second column.

Differentiation
Low Attainers – Discuss their story plan with an adult, who either supports writing or writes for children.
High Attainers – Many high attainers will be aware of and use speech punctuation with some degree of accuracy. Give children Copymaster 55 with speech punctuation deleted and ask them to put it in the correct place.

Whole class
Finish reading 'Because of Figs' to the class.

Lesson 2

Whole class

Look at plans that two of the class made for their story. Ask their permission first. Discuss how these would make interesting stories. Compare the events with the stories you have read. Ask the children to think how one of the stories could be started in an interesting way. Will you start with the setting, introduce a character, hint at a problem or start with some dialogue? Write onto a board one beginning sentence that introduces a character and one that describes a setting, re-read, both and discuss. Ask the children to vote for the beginning sentence they like best.

Group and independent work
Children finish planning and then write the beginning of

their stories. Tell them to think carefully about the first sentence. Remind them to re-read as they write.

Differentiation
Low Attainers – Use a storyboard to illustrate the first two events in the story and write a caption to go with the first picture.
High Attainers – Support this group in the completion of their story plan and the beginning of their stories. Discuss interesting first sentences and how they set the scene for the rest of the story and make the reader want to continue reading.

Whole class
Children sit in a circle. Go around the circle and ask children to read aloud their first sentence only. Discuss the range of beginnings. Decide on which are the most effective.

Lesson 3

Whole class

Show the children Copymaster 56. Tell them that you started to write your story but you were very tired and made a lot of mistakes. Ask the children to read the beginning of your story with a partner and find two mistakes or things that could be improved. Organise children into mixed ability pairs for this activity. Improve the writing, taking ideas from the children. Re-read the improved version together. Ask pairs to think what could happen next. Write the next couple of sentences with help from the class.

Group and independent work

Children continue writing their stories. Tell them to re-read their work before they begin.

Differentiation

Low Attainers – Help children to structure text to go with their second picture in their storyboard sequence. Encourage children to re-read what they wrote yesterday.

Whole class

Ask children how they think their work is going so far. What are the problems of being an author? What do you need to think about?

Lesson 4

Whole class

Write on the board some inappropriate story endings, e.g.
• *. . . and they all lived happily ever after.*
• *. . . and they had tea and went to bed.*
Discuss what is wrong with these endings. Recap on the work you have done on story endings during the year. Read one or two appropriate story endings from class texts. Discuss why these are better.

Group and independent work

Children continue to write their stories. Support a group by encouraging children to re-read their work. Discuss what has happened in the story and what will happen next. Refer to the plan. Highlight spelling and grammatical errors as you read work with children.

Differentiation

Low Attainers – Give children some simple texts and ask them to look at the ending of the stories. They might be able to use some of the ideas to make their story better.

Whole class

Ask for a volunteer to read their work so far.
Tell the children that they must think when they go home how they want to end their story for the lesson tomorrow.

Lesson 5

Whole class

Tell children that they are going to start their writing straight away. The aim is to give children longer to finish their stories and also to allow you to work with two guided writing groups to support the children's writing.

Group and independent work

Work with groups to support the writing and completion of the story.

Differentiation

Low Attainers – Use adult help to support children in completing text for their storyboard.

Whole class

Evaluate the work for the week. Give the children 'time out' to discuss what was enjoyable and what was difficult. Make a note on the board. Tell the children that next week they are going to look at their stories again and prepare them in book form.

Theme 8) Extended stories (week 3)

The literacy work this week involves completing and preparing stories to a standard where they can be presented to others. Ideally this will be in book form. Some children might re-draft their work, or some of their work. You might want some work to be word-processed. It will be useful to enlist the help of other adults to help children with preparing and making their books.

Objectives
Text level
• 10 To write sustained stories using knowledge of story elements.

Sentence level
• 1 To read aloud with intonation and expression appropriate to the grammar and punctuation.

Resources
Author details from week 1.
Copymaster 57. Homework 28.
Books *e.g. folded sugar paper* for completed work.

Assessment
At the end of this theme is the pupil able to:
• utilise thier knowledge of story elements to create their own sustained piece of story writing?

Lesson 1

Whole class

Talk to the class about what they need to do in order to make their stories special, so that other people will want to read them. Make a list of jobs that have to be done on a large piece of paper. *e.g. copy out neatly, stick author details into book.* Tell the children that they will need to work through the points on the list this week.

Group and independent work
Tell children to read through their work, noting any comments and corrections you have added to the work. There will probably be some children who have not finished writing their stories. If possible organise support for this group.

Differentiation
High Attainers – Support high attainers in starting the drafting process.
Low Attainers – Encourage children to read their story board stories, with adult support if available

Whole class
Low attainers read their work to the rest of the class. Comment on clear sequencing of the story and interesting or exciting events.

Lesson 2

Whole class

Show and read beginnings of some work in progress. Praise neat handwriting. Highlight any letters or joins that you have noticed children are not forming correctly. Demonstrate correct formation. Use whiteboards for children to practise. Observe formation. Show the children an illustration from a familiar story. Ask the children what the picture is telling you. Read the text that accompanies the picture and discuss the link between written text and illustration.
Look at sketches of illustrations from week 2 homework, linked to the work read. Discuss content of illustrations and make sure they will be linked to the text.

Group and independent work
Children work on presenting stories. Children will be:
• writing out drafted work;
• word processing;
• drawing illustrations.

Differentiation
Low Attainers – Copy text from storyboard into book or cut and paste storyboard sequence into book before illustrating

Whole class
Ask for volunteers from the class to show one illustration and read the accompanying text. Ask the rest of the class to check that the two are linked.

Lesson 3
Whole class

Remind children that you started this work by looking at the front covers of two books. Tell them that they will have to think about a title and illustration for the front of their book. Show children an enlarged copy of Copymaster 57. Ask the children to look at the sheet and put their hands up if they can tell you what is written on the list. Use titles that children know and ask the children if they can name the author of each book. Pick one or two examples of titles and ask the children

what the title tells you. Look at the books for the chosen titles and discuss how the illustration on the front cover supports and adds to the written title. Ask children for ideas for titles for their books. Write some examples on the board. Add title and front cover illustration to the list of jobs to be completed.

Group and independent work
Continue work on presenting stories as in Lesson 2. Encourage children to re-read the text before they draw the illustrations.

Lesson 4
Whole class

Tell the children that today they must finish their books and practise reading their stories so that they can share them with other children tomorrow. Pick several examples of work nearing completion. Read these examples to the class putting in the appropriate expression. Ask children why expression is important when reading to an audience. Re-read the beginning of

one piece of work with no expression. Ask the children how this this makes them feel about the story.

Group and independent work
Support groups in finishing their books. Children will be working on a variety of tasks and groups may need to be organised accordingly.

Whole class
Children sit in a circle with their work. Ask children to read their work to themselves. Support low attainers.

Lesson 5
Whole class

Organise children into mixed ability pairs. Tell the children to read their stories to each other using expression and making the story sound interesting. Tell the children to think of one positive comment about their partner's work beginning 'I like – story because …'. Ask children to share their comments with the rest of the class. (Try to have organised a programme for the

children to present their work so that all children have an opportunity to share their stories. This may mean that children have to go to a number of different classes during the day.)
Clear surfaces so that children can display their books around the room. Tell children to walk around, read and look at each other's work.
Come together and evaluate the work. Sit in a circle and think of positive comments about the work you have seen.

Theme 9) Information texts (week one)

Objectives
Text level

- 13 To understand the distinction between fact and fiction and to use the terms 'fact', 'fiction' and 'non-fiction' appropriately;
- 15 To use a contents page and index to find their way about a text;
- 16 To scan a text to find specific sections;
- 17 To skim-read title, contents page, illustrations, chapter headings and sub-headings to speculate what a book might be about;
- 18 To evaluate the usefulness of a text for its purpose;

Resources
A range of animal related non-fiction texts.

A non-fiction big book related to animals. Copymaster 58, Copymaster 59. Homework 29.

Resource preparation
Tell the children that you are going to be doing some work on animals and you would like them to choose their favourite animals and begin to collect information on that particular animal.
Set up a class display of animal related non-fiction texts.

Assessment
At the end of this theme is the pupil able to:
- understand the difference between the terms 'fact' and 'fiction';
- use the contents page of a non-fiction text;
- skim-read a text and speculate what it might be about?

Lesson 1
Whole class

Begin this unit by introducing the children to the terms 'fact' and 'fiction'. Write the terms on the board and explain their meanings. Write down three statements which are fact and three which are fiction. The fiction statements can be opinion, *e.g. I think our school is fun.* Ask the children to identify those statements which are fact, those which are fiction, and those which give an opinion. Put the children into mixed ability pairs and give each pair a whiteboard. Ask each pair to write down a simple statement which is factual, *e.g. a dog has four legs.* Ask the children to show their statements and check that each pair has given a fact. Repeat this with a fictional statement. Show the children an enlarged version of Copymaster 58 containing 'fact' and 'fiction'

statements. Read through the statements with the children and sort two or three of them into fact or fiction.

Group and independent work
Ask the children to sort the remaining statements into 'fact' or 'fiction' columns, then ask them to add some more of their own statements into each column.

Differentiation
Low Attainers – Give the children a shortened list of 'fact' and 'fiction' statements cut into strips and ask children to sort them into 'fact' and 'fiction'.
High Attainers – Ask the children to write four fact and four fiction statements onto strips of paper. Tell them to swap their statements with a friend and ask them to sort the statements into 'fact' and 'fiction'.

Lesson 2
Whole class

Recap on the terms 'fact' and 'fiction' with the children. Ask the children to brainstorm fiction books and non-fiction books they know. Show the children the non-fiction big book with the title covered up. Ask them to look at the illustration and guess whether it is a fiction or non-fiction text. How do they know? Can anyone explain the purpose of a non-fiction text? Do we have to read the whole text as we do with a story? Ask the children to identify the subject of the text from the front cover only. Can anyone guess what the title of the book might be? Turn to the contents page. Ask the children to explain how to use this page. Model this with the children, locating parts of interest to the children. Select an interesting page with the children and read it with them. Ask the children if they can give you three facts from this particular page. Model the process of writing the three facts, reinforcing the use of full stops and capital letters.

Group and independent work
Put a selection of non-fiction texts on each table. Ask the children to select a book, record the title and use the contents page to select a page in the book of interest to them. Ask the children to record three facts from that page.

Differentiation
Low Attainers – This activity can be completed as a group with adult support. Read the text to the children and ask them to state three facts from that page.
High Attainers – Ask the group to repeat the activity with several texts. Encourage them to skim-read their texts to locate their facts.

Whole class
Ask some children to read out the facts they have found from the book. Can the rest of the class guess the title of the book they have selected?

Lesson 3

Whole class

Recap on the term 'non-fiction' with the children and show them the non-fiction big book. Ask the class for a volunteer to model how to use the contents page of the non-fiction book. Select a new page from the non-fiction big book that has been pre-selected by you and read it with the children. Have three questions prepared which can be answered using that particular page of the book. Ask the children to locate the answers in the text. These can be underlined if you use a sheet of acetate over the top of the text. Focus on the use of sub-headings to help children to locate the correct section on the page. Use the shared writing process to model how to answer the questions using complete sentences. Focus on the use of the question in the answer, e.g. *How many legs does a dog have? A dog has . . .*

Group and independent work

Organise the children into mixed ability pairs. Give pairs a copy of a different page from a non-fiction text. Invent some questions that can be answered by reading the text. Ask the children to read the text together and answer the question. Reinforce the use of complete sentences.

Differentiation

Low Attainers – You may wish to select an easier text extract for this group with accompanying questions.
High Attainers – Ask the children to write an extra question for their partner to answer when they have completed the task.

Whole class

Ask pairs of children to give their answers to the set questions. Focus on whether the children have used the question to form part of their answers.

Lesson 4

Whole class

Show the children a non-fiction big book and ask a child to demonstrate how to use the contents page to the rest of the class. Ask the children if there are any other sections which tell us what the book contains. Look at the index. Ask the children to identify similarities between the index page and the contents page. Reinforce the use of alphabetical ordering when looking at this page. Ask the children to demonstrate how to find certain sections by using the index page. Show them the glossary section in the book. (There may not be one, in which case you will need a different non-fiction text for this.) Explain to the children that a glossary is very similar to a dictionary as it gives you definitions to tricky words in the text. Read some of the definitions. Reinforce the use of alphabetical ordering when reading this page. Ask the children to compare the glossary definitions to the dictionary definitions. Are they written in a similar style? Draw attention to the use of direct language. Choose a word which relates to a relevant topic, or a literacy hour term such as 'antonym' or 'compound word'. Use the shared writing process to write a glossary definition for that particular word.

Group and independent work

Give the children a selection of topic-related words or literacy hour terms which they will be able to define (you may wish to differentiate these). Ask the children to order them alphabetically and define them. Remind them of the type of language used in definitions.

Differentiation

Low Attainers – Make sure this group has three or four words they are able to define. They can define the words as a group with adult support and arrange their words in alphabetical order.
High Attainers – Give this group some more complex words to define. Can they define each word using only one or two sentences?

Whole class

Ask some children to read out their glossary definitions. Can the rest of the class guess the word which they were defining? Focus on appropriate language use.

Lesson 5

Whole class

Recap on using non-fiction texts with the children. Use a range of books and ask the children if they can identify the content of the texts just by looking at the front cover. Read the children a contents page from one of the books. Can they identify what the book could be about? Look at the use of sub-headings. How do they help us to use the book more effectively? Ask some children to identify where on the page you would find certain information using the sub-headings. Look for other key features. What other things do authors include on the page to make the books more interesting, *e.g. fact files, illustrations?* Make a class list of additional features. Show the children an enlarged copy of Copymaster 59 and use it to review one of the non-fiction texts you have looked at as a class.

Group and independent work

Give groups of children a selection of non-fiction texts. Ask them to work individually or in pairs to look for key features in some of the texts. Give each child or pair a copy of Copymaster 59 to complete.

Differentiation

Low Attainers – Ask the children to select their favourite non-fiction text, draw the front cover of the book and write a sentence about it.
High Attainers – Complete an extra box which identifies suggestions for improving that particular text.

Whole class

Ask the children to select their favourite non-fiction text and explain to the rest of the class which features made that book interesting. Add any new features the children have found to the class list.

Theme 10 Information texts (week two)

Objectives

Text level

- 14 To pose questions and record these in writing, prior to reading non-fiction and to find answers;
- 19 To make simple notes from non-fiction texts, *e.g. key words and phrases, page references, headings,* to use in subsequent writing;
- 20 To write non-fiction texts, using texts read as models for own writing.

Sentence level

- 6 To turn statements into questions, learning a range of 'wh' words typically used to open question, and to add question marks.

Resources

A selection of non-fiction texts relating to animals for the children to refer to (ensure that the children have the texts they will need to complete their own piece of non-fiction writing on animals).
'Post-it' notes.
A non-fiction big book.
Copymaster 60. Homework 30.
A sheet of acetate to cover the page of a non-fiction book.

Resource preparation

Prepare two questions which can be answered using the non-fiction big book. Enlarge a version of Copymaster 55.

Assessment

At the end of this theme is the pupil able to:

- use and spell a range of 'wh' words when asking questions, prior to reading non-fiction texts;
- make notes from non-fiction texts;
- write their own non-fiction text based on models from their reading?

Lesson 1

Whole class

Put the children into two teams. Tell the children that you are going to describe an animal to them and the first person to guess the animal that you are describing wins a point. Describe a range of animals to the class making the clues progressively easier.
e.g. You may see me in the zoo: I have four legs→ I live in a hot country→ I can run very fast→ I have spots.
Keep scores for each team and find the winner after three or four animals. Ask the children to tell you the name of an animal which has not been described so far. Using the shared writing process, ask the children to help you to write a series of descriptive sentences for that animal. Encourage the children to make the descriptions progressively easier. Focus on the use of full stops and capital letters.

Group and independent work

Give each child some 'post-it' notes. Ask the children to think of an animal to describe and draw it in their book. Cover the drawing with a 'post-it' note and write some sentences underneath to describe that animal. The children can repeat this describing a range of animals.

Differentiation

Low Attainers – This group can draw their animals and describe them using simple repeated sentences on prompt cards, *e.g. I am ...*
High Attainers – Encourage this group to ensure that their descriptions become progressively easier. Ask them to extend some sentences using 'but', *e.g. I have stripes but they are not black and white.*

Whole class

Ask some children to read out the sentences they have written to describe their animals. Can the rest of the class guess which animal they are describing?

Lesson 2

Whole class

Write a statement on the board, such as 'A cat has four legs'. Ask the children if anyone can turn your statement into a question. Scribe the question underneath your original statement. Repeat this with a different statement but ask the children if they can think of a question which begins with a 'wh' word. Ask the children to brainstorm any other words they think of which often begin a question. Make a class list. Focus on those words which begin with 'wh' explaining to the children that the 'h' in the word is a silent letter. Can they think of any more words beginning with or containing 'wh' sound? Add these words to the list. Tell the children which animals they are going to write about. Explain to the children that they need to have some ideas before they start their writing. Choose an animal and model how to brainstorm a list of questions related to that particular animal, *e.g. Where does it live? What does it eat?* Draw attention to the use of any 'wh' words here.

Group and independent work

Ask the children to write the name of their animal in the middle of their page and brainstorm a range of questions related to their chosen animal. Explain to the children that they are going to try to find the answers to their questions in the next session, using non-fiction texts. Encourage the correct spelling of all the 'wh' words which they have encountered today.

Differentiation

Low Attainers – Work as a group choosing one animal between them and brainstorming questions. This can be recorded with adult support.
High Attainers – Encourage this group to write more complex sentences and ensure the correct spelling of 'wh' words.

Lesson 3

Whole class

Show the children the non-fiction big book. Recap on using the contents page to locate various sections within the text. Write a question on the board which can be answered by using the text. Ask the children if anyone can demonstrate how to locate the answer to the question using the big book. Reinforce the use of the contents page and skim reading when locating the answer. Explain to the children that they need only make notes to answer their questions today. Using the shared writing process, model how to answer the question in note form. Begin by using a complete sentence. Ask the children to eliminate any words which are unnecessary, leaving only the key words needed to answer the question. Repeat this process using the second question.

Group and independent work

Provide the children with a range of non-fiction texts relating to animals. Most of the children should have collected their own texts to use. Ask the children to locate the answers to as many questions as they can, explaining that they may not be able to find the answers to all the questions. Ask the children to answer each question in note form, extracting the key points only.

Differentiation

Low Attainers – Locate the answers to their group questions with adult support if appropriate. The answers can be recorded pictorially, adding key words and phrases.
High Attainers – Encourage this group to include as much detail as they can find when answering their questions, trying to give reasons behind the answers.

Whole class

Ask some children to report to the class on their findings. Focus on whether the children have recorded their answers in note form. Draw attention to those children who have included more details in their answers.

Lesson 4

Whole class

Make sure the children have their notes which they made in the previous session with them. Recap on the class list made on features of non-fiction texts, showing examples of these in texts. Tell the children that today they are going to begin to write their non-fiction page and that you are going to put all their pages together to make a book. Ask the children to help you to make a list of things to remember, *e.g. begin with a title, use of sub-headings and use of illustrations in their work.* What things do we need to remember with each section, *e.g. the title needs to stand out, the sub-headings need to be clear.* Tell the rest of the class to comment on their choices. Using the shared writing process, model for the children how to record sub-headings on Copymaster 60. With a partner ask the children to discuss which key features of non-fiction writing they will use in their work. Model the recording of this on Copymaster 60.

Group and independent work

Give each child a copy of Copymaster 60. Ask them to use this to plan their piece of non-fiction writing. Give each child a large sheet of paper. Tell them to begin with the title of their piece of non-fiction writing when they are ready.

Differentiation

Low Attainers – Ask each child to begin work on a particular section of the group page using illustrations.
High Attainers – This group can be encouraged to include more than five sub-headings in their work. Encourage them to check and evaluate each other's sub-headings and key features.

Whole class

Put the children into pairs and ask partners to evaluation their friend's sub-headings and check the correct spelling of 'wh' words. Ask some children to report back to the rest of the class.

Lesson 5

Whole class

Tell the children that they are going to begin to write the main part of their text today. Show the children the non-fiction big book and tell them that you are going to use the book to find types of words that are used when writing information texts. Identify the key differences between the way a non-fiction book is written and a storybook is written. Put the acetate over a page in the non-fiction big book. Read the page with the children and ask them to identify key words and phrases which begin sentences and join two sentences together. Make a class list for the children to refer to when writing their piece of text. Put the children into pairs and give each pair a non-fiction book and a whiteboard. Ask pairs to find at least one more key phrase which begins or joins sentences.

Group and independent work

Ask the children to continue working on their non-fiction writing, encouraging them to use the bank of words and phrases written during the whole class session.

Differentiation

Low Attainers – Allow this group to continue working on their group writing.
High Attainers – Encourage this group to extend their sentences using the key words and phrases found during the whole class session.

Whole class

Ask the children to bring their piece of non-fiction to the circle. Tell any children who have looked at the same animal to sit together. Give each of the children a number starting from two and ask them to put that number on the bottom of their page. If some children have chosen the same animal give them one number only. Make a class contents page for the book using the children's numbers. The children's work can be made into a class book of animals. You may want to spend some time devising a glossary and an index to add to the book.

Stories with familiar settings

A time when I was jealous was when

_____

_____

_____

_____

I felt jealous because

_____

_____

_____

_____

I solved the problem by

_____

_____

_____

_____

Afterwards I felt

_____

_____

_____

_____

Stories with familiar settings

1	2

3	4

Stories with familiar settings

jump	help	stop
hope	cook	hop
cry	chop	roll
walk	dance	reach
drag	push	change
dress	pick	rest
rescue	thump	clean
wash	brush	try

Stories with familiar settings

This is the _____

who _____

and _____

_____

_____

_____

_____

Stories with familiar settings

One day Mog chased a butterfly.

_____

_____

Mrs Thompson put Mog in the basket.

_____

_____

Suddenly all the animals were going wild!

_____

_____

In the morning her paw was no longer sore.

_____

Stories with familiar settings

heal	please	keep
field	he	see	sweep
cheese	stream	chief
reach	speed	mean
heel	green	speak
use	feet	

Stories with familiar settings

My story is called

_____

The settings in my story are _____

_____

_____

_____

My pet needs to go to the vet because _____

_____

_____

_____

This was caused by _____

_____

_____

_____

The problem at the vet's is _____

_____

_____

_____

The problem is solved by _____

_____

_____

_____

Stories with familiar settings

once upon a tim there was a cat called corky and he licked to climb the tree in the back gardon. one sunny afternoon he was busy climbin his tree and he slipped on a soggy leaf and fel to the grownd he meowed and meowed and no-one herd him. corky laid very still his leg was very sore and he could not walk and the cat from next door cam strolling past corky meowed very loudly and the cat from next heard him and ran over to see wot the problem was. corky told the cat that he had hurt his leg and could not walk and the cat from next dor ran off to get help.

PURR!

Stories with familiar settings

Title of story	When does the story begin?	When does the story end?
1		
2		
3		
4		

Stories with familiar settings

Mr. Gumpy told:
- the children not to squabble
- the rabbit not to hop
- the cat not to chase the rabbit
- the dog not to tease the cat
- the pig not to muck about
- the sheep not to bleat
- the chickens not to flap
- the calf not to trample
- the goat not to kick

For a little while they all went along happily but then . . .

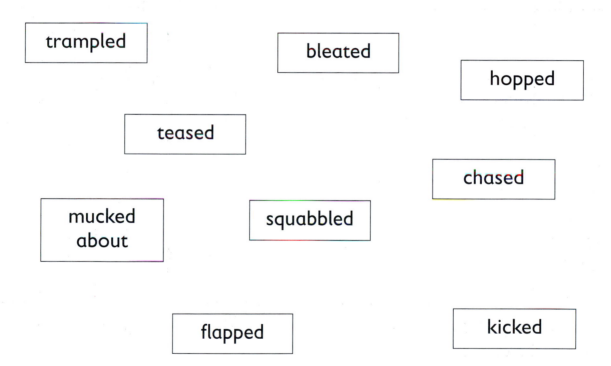

Stories with familiar settings

	Mr. Gumpy's Outing	Mr. Gumpy's Motor Car
characters		
setting		
problem		
what happens to the characters		
ending		
which story is the most interesting?		
why?		

Stories with familiar settings

1 Where did Mr. Gumpy want to go?	**2** Who wanted to go with him?
3 What was the problem?	**4** What happened?
5 What did they do?	**6** What happened in the end?

Poems with familiar settings

Night-time, Fright-time

Night-time, fright-time,
Please leave on the light time.

Night-time. Shadows creep.
Floorboards creak. Can't sleep.

Night-time, fright-time,
Please leave on the light time.

Night-time. Darkness hides.
Goblin chuckles. Ghost glides.

Night-time, fright-time,
Please leave on the light time.

Night-time, fear time,
Something's creeping near time.

Night-time, fright-time,
PLEASE LEAVE ON THE LIGHT TIME!

John Foster

Poems with familiar settings

radiators	whine
street lights	drip
goblin	flicker
taps	creak
cupboards	moan
cats	squeak
doors	bang

Poems with familiar settings

AFTER DARK

Outside after dark
trains hum and traffic-lights wink
after dark, after
dark.

In here after dark
curtains shake and
cupboards creak
after dark, after
dark.

Under the covers
after dark
I twiddle my toes and hug my pillow
after dark, after dark.

Michael Rosen

Instructions

Fruit cocktail

This delicious drink is simple to make and is deliciously cool on a hot summer's day.

You will need:

- 2 tall glasses
- fresh orange juice
- lemonade
- 1 lemon
- 1 orange
- ice cubes

What to do:

- First, pour half a glass of orange juice into each glass.

- Next, top both glasses up with lemonade.

- Take the orange and the lemon and cut them into slices.

- Add a slice of lemon and a slice of orange to each glass.

- Finally put a couple of ice cubes into each glass.

If you are having a party, why not make this drink in a large jug with lots of lemon, orange and ice!

Instructions

1. Take a sheet of newspaper and fold it in half.

2. With the folded edge on top, fold each corner into the centre to make a triangle shape.

3. You should be left with two flaps on the bottom. Fold one of the flaps up, then turn the hat over and fold the other flap up.

4. Pick the hat up and place your hand in the centre of the hat between the two sheets of paper. Pull the two sides apart to make a hat shape.

5. Wear your new hat with pride!

Traditional stories

Name of character _____

In the bag we have _____

_____

and _____ .

What do they look like?

_____

_____

What do they say?

How do they feel?

Traditional stories

Run, run as fast as you can,

you can't catch me I'm the Gingerbread Man.

I'll huff and I'll puff and

I'll blow your house down.

Who's been eating

my porridge.

Grandmother,

let down your golden hair.

what big eyes you have!

Mirror, mirror on the wall,

who is the fairest one of all?

Rapunzel, Rapunzel,

Who's that crossing

Who will help me

my bridge.

cook the cakes?

Traditional stories

My favourite traditional tale is ....

....

....

The setting/s for this story is/are ....

....

....

The main characters in the story are ....

....

....

My favourite part of this story is ....

....

....

Draw a picture.

Traditional stories

WANTED

_____

Name: _____

Age: _____

Description: _____

_____

_____

_____

Warning: _____

_____

_____

_____

Reward: _____

Traditional stories

Red Riding Hood are going to her Grandma's house.

They is going to bake a pie.

The wolf have got a hungry tummy.

The trees has scary faces.

'I is going to eat you!' shouted the wolf.

They was very brave.

The wolf were sorry.

'The woodcutter are out here!' said Grandma and Red Riding Hood.

They all goes home for a nice cup of tea.

Traditional stories

MY HERO

My hero is called ....

His/her special power is ....

My hero will save Grandma by ....

....

....

....

....

....

....

....

Traditional stories

'All the better to eat you with!' snarled the wolf. Suddenly the wolf pulled the covers bac and leapt owt of bed.

In a flash the door burst open and in came Red Riding Hood's mother.

'I is here to save the day!' shoutid her Mum.

'I are super Mum!'

Red Riding Hood's mum am dressed in blue shiny tights and a brite red cloak.

Red Riding Hood couldn't believe her eyes!

she stood and watched as her mum picked the wolf up wiv her bare hands, carried him two the door and threw him up into the air.

She throwed him so hard that he bounced of the moon and come hurtling back towards earf.

The wolf hit the earth wiv such forse that he made a huge howl in the ground and were never seen again.

Evrybody cheered, Super Mum did saved the day!

Traditional stories from other cultures

The King with Dirty Feet

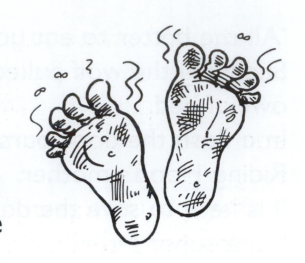

Once upon a time there was a king. He lived in a hot, dusty village. He had everything he wanted and was very happy. But there was one thing that this king hated and that was bathtime.

Perhaps he was a bit like you? This king had not washed for a week, he had not washed for a month, he had not washed for a whole year. He had begun to smell. He smelt underneath his arms, in between his toes, behind his ears and up his nose. He was the smelliest king there had ever been. His servants were all very polite about it, but nobody liked to be in the same room as him. Until one day the smell became too much for even the king himself, and he said rather sadly, 'I think it is time I had a bath.'

He walked slowly to the river. The villagers whispered, 'The king's going to have a bath!' and they rushed down to the river bank to get the best view.

Traditional stories from other cultures

'Gabu,' boomed the king, 'the king has had a bath, the king is clean but the earth is dirty. There is dust everywhere. You must clean the earth so there is no more dust and my feet stay clean.'

'Yes, Your Majesty,' replied Gabu.

'You have three days in which to rid the land of dust, and if you fail do you know what will happen to you?' asked the king.

'No, Your Majesty.'

'ZUT!' cried the king.

'ZUT?' said Gabu. 'What is ZUT?'

'ZUT is the sound of your head being chopped off.'

Gabu began to cry.

'Don't waste time, Gabu. Rid the land of dust at once.'

The king marched back to his palace.

'I must put my thinking cap on,' said Gabu and he put his head in his hands and began to think.

from *The King with Dirty Feet*,
retold by Robert Clayton

Traditional stories from other cultures

Planning your writing

Title: How _____ stole the fire.

Who had the fire?

Where did they live?

How was the fire stolen?

Which animals helped to steal the fire?

1 _____

2 _____

3 _____

What happened at the end of the story?

Traditional stories from other cultures

_____ stole the fire.	_____ stole the fire from _____.
_____ lived _____.	_____ helped to steal the fire.
_____ helped to steal the fire.	What happened at the end of the story?

Traditional stories from other cultures

How do the stories end?

How Rabbit stole the fire

The sky people _____ .

Rabbit _____ .

Last sentence:

_____

Rainbow Bird

What happened to Crocodile?

_____

What happened to Rainbow Bird?

_____

Think of words to describe how the stories end.

_____

_____

_____

_____

_____

_____

Poems with predictable and patterned language

Morning

Morning comes
    with a milk-float jiggling

Morning comes
    with a milkman whistling

Morning comes
    with empties clinking

Morning comes
    with alarm-clock ringing

Morning comes
    with toaster popping

Morning comes
    with letters dropping

Morning comes
    with kettle singing

Morning comes
    with just me listening.

Morning comes to drag me out of bed
    – Boss-Woman Morning.

Grace Nichols

97

Poems with predictable and patterned language

Title: _____

What is the poem about?

_____

_____

Choose two phrases that you like

1 _____

2 _____

Note 3 things about the shape or rhyme or pattern of the poem.

1 _____

2 _____

3 _____

Poems with predictable and patterned language

I'm just going out for a moment

I'm just going out for a moment.
Why?
To make a cup of
tea.
Why?
Because I'm thirsty.
Why?
Because it's hot.
Why?
Because the sun's
shining.
Why?
Because it's summer.
Why?
Because that's when it is.
Why?
Why don't you stop saying why?
Why?
Tea-time why.
High-time-you-stopped-saying-why time.

What?

Michael Rosen

Poems with predictable and patterned language

I'm just going out for a moment

I'm just going out for a moment.

Why?

Why?

Why?

Why?

Why?

Why?

Why?

Why?

High-time-you-stopped-saying-why-time.

What?

Poems with predictable and patterned language

My Sweet

Shall I tell you about the sweet
I'm going to invent?

When you first pop it in
you feel ten feet all.
You look around the
world as if you own it.

And when you start to
chew
your arms go Zing!
and your legs go Zong!
They're as strong as
cranes.

And when you swallow
my sweet
you can see over hills and seas
and into the tiniest insect's home.

You're a giant
with magic eyes.

Would you like one?

Richard Brown

Explanations

A butterfly lays its eggs on a leaf.

The eggs hatch out into caterpillars. The caterpillars eat the leaves and grow bigger and bigger.

When the caterpillars are big enough, they spin a cocoon around themselves. They have now become chrysalis.

After a few weeks the chrysalis begins to break and out comes a butterfly.

The butterfly sits on a leaf and waits for its wings to dry before flying away.

Dictionaries

A

G

K

Q

U   Z

Different stories by the same author

Comparing the settings of two Martin Waddell stories

Title		
Author		
Setting		
Description		
Similarities		
Differences		

Extension: Why do you think Martin Waddell chose those particular settings for the two stories?

Different stories by the same author

A review of ....

by ....

book cover

Price

Rating: 1 star 2 stars 3 stars 4 stars 5 stars

This story is about ....

....

....

....

My favourite part of the story is ....

....

....

I would recommend this story to ....

....

....

....

Different stories by the same author

Character?	
Book	
Appearance	
Personality	
Similarities	
Differences	

Different stories by the same author

I would/would not recommend Martin Waddell to you.

The characters in his stories are _____

_____

_____

_____

His stories are set _____

_____

_____

_____

The themes he uses are _____

_____

_____

_____

I think you would particularly enjoy

_____ because _____

_____

_____

_____

_____

_____

Riddles

I'm a kind of fish but I don't live in a bowl.
I have lots of very sharp teeth.
I have a big pointed fin on my back.
I'm as long as two cars.

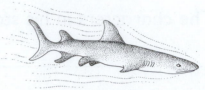

A shark

I'm a kind of cat.
I have a long curvy tail.
I have stripy fur.
I live in the jungle.

A tiger

I have wings like a parrot but I can't fly.
My favourite food is fish.
I have a pointed beak.
I live near the icy South Pole.

A penguin

I'm a kind of dog like a puppy.
I have pointed ears.
I have a bushy tail.
I live in a den underground.

A fox

Riddles

My first is in *book* but not in cover,
My second is in *sister* but not in
brother,
My third is in *rain* but not in sun,
My fourth is in *bread* but not in bun,
My whole is a creature. Watch me fly,
Soaring in an azure sky.

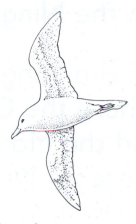

A bird

I was round and small like a pearl,
Then long and slender and brave as an earl,
Since, like a hermit I live in a cell,
And now like a rogue, in the wide world I dwell.

First an egg,
Then a silkworm,
Then a cocoon,
Lastly, a moth.

Humorous Verse

On the Ning Nang Nong

On the Ning Nang Nong
Where the Cows go Bong!
And the Monkeys all say Boo!
There's a Nong Nang Ning
Where the trees go Ping!
And the tea pots Jibber Jabber Joo.
On the Nong Ning Nang
All the mice go Clang!
And you just can't catch 'em when they do!
So it's Ning Nang Nong!
Cows go Bong!
Nong Nang Ning!
Trees go Ping!
Nong Ning Nang!
The Mice go Clang!
What a noisy place to belong,
Is the Ning Nang Ning Nang Nong!

Spike Milligan

Humorous verse

Mary Mary quite contrary,
How does your garden grow?
With silver bells and cockle shells
and pretty maids all in a row.

Humorous verse

Mary Mary quite contrary
What does your garden hide?
Beetles and bugs
Slithery slugs
And shells with snails inside.

Humorous verse

A fly and a flea flew up a flue,
Said the fly to the flea, 'What shall we
do?'
'Let's fly,' said the flea.
'Let's flee,' said the fly
So they fluttered and flew up a flaw in
the flue.

Did he say I said you said she said that?
He said you said I said she said that!
Well I didn't!

Extended stories

Author	Information about author	Title of book	One story or collection	Why I would read/ not read the book

Extended stories

	Book 1	Book 2
Title		
Characters		
Setting		
Problem		
What happened next		
How does the story end		

Extended stories

Title _____

I like/do not like this story because _____

_____

_____

I thought the _____ could be improved.

_____

_____

_____

I would/would not recommend this book to _____

_____

_____

_____

I would/would not want to read this book again because _____

_____

_____

_____

I would give this book _____ marks out of ten.

Extended stories

Because of Figs

In the summer I like to lie in the grass and look at clouds and eat figs. Figs are soft and purple and delicious. Their juice runs all over my face, and I eat them till I'm so full I can't eat any more.

Because of figs I got a strange birthday present, and because of that birthday present I had some trouble. This is what happened.

It all started long ago when I had my fourth birthday. My father came home from work and said, 'I have something for you Julian! Go and look in the car'.

Extended stories

Upstairs and Upstairs

As soon as Rosie and Ella saw the house they knew something was missing. The house was tall and thin. It stood on the pavement.

Rosie said, 'Where is the garden?'

'Gardens are at the back,' Ella said.

'It's got a lot of windows,' Daddy said.

They stood on the street and counted: one door and seven windows.

There was no garden at the front of the house, only a paved place for the dustbin and three steps to the door. The top step was where a milk bottle lived. It looked as if it had lived there for a long time.

Extended stories

It was sonday evening and i sat in my bedroom thinking about school. How could I get out of the test. I knew I could not do it.

Huey, mum and dad were downstairs wotching television.

'Julian, what are you doing' said dad.

Nothing, I'll be down in a minute, I said.

Perhaps I could pretend I was ill lots of children had got chicken pox this term but I would need some spots.

I went into the bathroom and saw just the thing.

Extended stories

The Twig Thing

This is the Bear and the Scary Night

Mr Gumpy's Outing

Mog and the Vee Eee Tee

Owl Babies

Where's Spot?

Goldilocks and the Three Bears

How Rabbit Stole the Fire

Information texts

Fact or fiction?

• A baby horse is called a puppy.

• A cat has sharp claws.

• A shark lives on the land.

• A cheetah can run very fast.

• Chickens give us milk.

• A dog lays eggs.

• A group of birds is called a flock.

• A baby cow is called a cowlet.

• An insect has six legs.

• A rabbit lives in a burrow.

• A horse can fly.

• Cats eyes glow in the dark.

• A zebra has black and white stripes.

125

Information texts

Can you find these things?

Book title	What is the book about	Contents Page	Index	Glossary	Any other key features	Your opinion of the book

Information texts

My non-fiction writing plan

My information plan is about

. . . .

My sub-headings will be:

1 . . . .

2 . . . .

3 . . . .

4 . . . .

5 . . . .

To make my non-fiction writing more interesting I will use these features:

1 . . . .

2 . . . .

3 . . . .

The literacy work this week has been based around a book called This is the Bear. The children have:
• Sequenced parts of the story in the correct order, adding their own words;
• Written about their own experiences of feeling jealous;
• Focused on the use of the past tense in their writing.

Can you add the suffix 'ed' to these words and put the words into a sentence?

jump _____   • _____

_____

show _____   • _____

_____

help _____   • _____

_____

play _____   • _____

_____

brush _____   • _____

_____

cook _____   • _____

_____

Can you think of any more words that you can add the suffix 'ed' to?

_____   _____

_____   _____

_____   _____

The literacy work this week has been based around the book 'This is the Bear and the Scary Night'. The children have:
- retold the story from the bear's point of view;
- written their own stories about being lost or feeling frightened in the same style of the book;
- investigated words with an 'ed' suffix.

On a separate sheet of paper design a front cover for your own book about feeling lost or frightened.

Don't forget to include these things;
- A bold title;
- An illustration which gives the reader a clue about the plot of the story;
- The author's and illustrator's names;
- The name of the publisher of your story.

Design a back cover to your book.

Don't forget to include these things;
- A blurb which gives a brief outline of your story;
- A newspaper review of your story;
- The bar code with an ISBN number.

Use some of your story books at home to give you some ideas for your front and back covers.

The literacy work this week has been based around the book 'Mog and the Vee Eee Tee'.
The children have:
• read part of the story and predicted how it might end;
• sequenced parts of the story;
• looked at words and phrases which begin or join sentences;
• looked at words which contain the long vowel phoneme 'ee'.

Sort these words into three columns according to their spelling pattern;

| speak | feed | meat | dream | field | feet |
| me | see | heat | behind | please | |

ee	ea	others

Now try and find some more words for each column.
Can you find any words, which sound the same but contain different spelling patterns? e.g. see/sea.

The literacy work this week has been concerned with writing stories with familiar settings. The children have:
- chosen a main character for their story;
- planned their stories using a given structure;
- written their own story based around the book 'Mog and the Vee Eee Tee';
- read through their stories checking for sense and correct use of punctuation.

Have a go at writing your own story with a familiar setting. Use this story starter to begin your story;

It was a cold and rainy night and the wind was howling outside the window. My family and I were sat on the sofa watching the television. Suddenly the lights went out and the strangest thing happened ...

Here are some things to remember when you are writing your story.

- Make sure your story has a problem.
- The end of the story should resolve the problem.
- Use some interesting words and phrases to begin and join sentences other than 'and'.
- Use full stops and capital letters in your work.
- Read through your story at the end and check spellings and punctuation.

Write on a separate sheet of paper.

The literacy work this week has been concerned with stories with familiar settings. The children have:
• compared oral recounts of the focus story with the text;
• thought about the sequence and time relationships of the story;
• sequenced two similar stories;
• investigated 'ed' past tense word endings.

Using your reading book or a favourite short story pick out the most important events and put them in order in the boxes below.

1	2
3	**4**
5	**6**

The literacy work this week has followed on from the previous week and we have continued to look at stories with familiar settings.
The children have:
• planned and written their own story in book form.

Show your story plan and story to an adult or older brother or sister.
• Tell them the story of *Mr. Gumpy's Outing*.
• Show them your story sequence and explain the six events.
• Read your story to them, remembering to put in expression.
• Let them read your story to you.

Then:
• In the box below say what you like best about your story and what you would like to write a story about next.
• Read the sentences to an adult or ask an adult to read them with you.

I like the characters in my story because _____

_____

I think the problem is good because _____

_____

I would like to write my next story about _____

_____

The literacy work this week has been concerned with poems with familiar settings. The children have:
• read and discussed two poems about night-time;
• used these poetry structures to substitute their own ideas and to write new lines.

Remember how we read the poems in class and put in the correct expression.

• Try to learn 'Night-time, Fright-time' so you can say the poem without looking at the words.

• Try writing out one of the verses without looking at the poem, then check to see if your version is correct.

The literacy work this week has been concerned with poems with familiar settings and follows on from the previous unit of work. The children have written their own poem called 'In bed at night' using ideas from the poems they brought home last week.

Read your poem to an adult and tell them how you developed the ideas during the week.

You can write lots of different poems in the same way.
Try to think of ideas for writing a poem about:

In the park on a sunny day I hear _____

_____

_____

In the park on a sunny day I see _____

_____

_____

In the park on a sunny day I feel _____

_____

_____

The literacy work this week has been concerned with instructions. The children have:
• read a range of instructions from a variety of sources;
• investigated the way in which instructions are written and how they are organised;
• given verbal instructions and recorded these in sentences.

How many different types of instructions can you find around your home?

Make a list of these.

Try to collect some examples of the instructions that you find and add them to our class display.

Here are some ideas to look for:

RECIPE BOOKS

MODEL KITS

ART AND CRAFT BOOKS

BOARD GAMES

See if you can find them in as many different places as possible.

Try to read and follow some of the instructions with an adult.

The literacy work this week has been concerned with writing instructions.
The children have:
- followed a set of instructions to make a paper hat;
- written their own instructions for a playground game using diagrams to make the instructions easier to read.

Ask an adult to help you make a glass of squash. Try writing a set of instructions for this.

Try to use these words when writing your instructions:

first	next	finally

after that	stir

Don't forget to use these!

- Title
- Numbers
- Diagrams
- Safety tips
- Full stops and capital letters

> The literacy work this week has been concerned with looking at characters in traditional stories.
> The children have:
> • described characters orally;
> • written simple descriptions of characters;
> • made lists of characteristics separating items in the list with commas.

Complete the sentences, making sure you use commas in the appropriate place.

In the story of Little Red Riding Hood the characters are _____

_____

_____

and _____ .

In the story of Goldilocks and the Three Bears the characters are

_____

_____

and _____ .

The literacy work this week has been concerned with traditional tales. Children have:
- read the story Little Red Riding Hood;
- looked at the settings in the story, thinking about which part of the story takes place in each setting;
- described the characters of the wolf and Little Red Riding Hood and the reasons why they act as they do in the story.

Choose your favourite traditional tale (other than Little Red Riding Hood).

How many settings are there in your story?

Draw each of the settings.

Can you think of some words to describe each setting?
Which part of the story takes place in each of the settings?

_____

_____

_____

_____

The literacy work this week has been concerned with traditional stories, children have:
- written a new ending to Little Red Riding Hood, inventing their own hero for the story
- focused on using the correct grammatical agreement e.g. I am/the children are.

Read these sentences. Can you spot the word which needs changing to make the sentence sound correct? Circle the words and write the correct ones below.

1 I is going to play in the park.

_____

2 My friend and I am going swimming in the sea.

_____

3 The children is going to make some cakes at school today.

_____

4 We was very pleased with our new classroom computer.

_____

5 Pizza are my favourite food.

_____

6 My mum are helping me with my homework.

_____

The literacy work this week has been concerned with a traditional story from another culture, with a particular focus on the characters in the story.
Children have:
- described characters in the story and compared them with characters they know from other stories;
- chosen appropriate words and looked at opposite characteristics;
- identified dialogue and the use of speech marks in the story and written their own speech bubble dialogue.

Using a traditional story, a favourite story or a reading book from school:

- Name 3 characters in the story and write one name at the top of each column;
- Find words or phrases in the text that describe the characters.
- Think of two more words or phrases and add to the list.

The literacy work this week has been concerned with traditional stories from other cultures with a particular focus on the story settings.
Children have:
- described story settings;
- compared the story settings;
- redescribed story settings in writing.

Add words and phrases to the text below that describes the wood where the prince lives. Draw a picture to go with your description.

Once upon a time there was a sad prince who lived in a _____ house in a country far away. When the prince stood at his window he could see _____ trees and a _____ river. The sky was always _____ because the sun had forgotten how to shine.

The literacy work this week has been concerned with writing a new version of a traditional story using the same setting as in How Rabbit Stole the Fire which we read last week.

Children have:
- planned their story;
- tried to include some description of the setting at the beginning of their story;
- thought about repetitive phrases to use in the story;
- thought about how traditional stories end.

Your child has brought their work home to share and talk about with you.

In order to give your child practice in re-telling and re-reading their own work:

• Discuss what the story is about before reading;

• Look at any illustrations;

• Ask your child to read the story to you or re-read it together.

> The literacy work this week has been concerned with poems with predictable and patterned language.
> The children have:
> • read and discussed poems;
> • substituted their own phrases within a class poem;
> • investigated how words are built through the joining of syllables
> • investigated and found compound words.

Using the Compound Word sheet you started in class:

• read the definition of a compound word;

• read the examples we have already found;

• find as many compound words as you can to add to your list.

You could look in:

• your reading book;

• a dictionary.

You could also:

• talk to an adult or older brother or sister.

Write your list of words here:

_____

_____

_____

_____

_____

_____

_____

_____

The literacy work this week has been concerned with poems with predictable and patterned language.
Children have:
- read and discussed poems;
- used the structure from two poems to write their own versions.

Read the rhyming poem you have been given. Ask an adult or an older brother or sister if you need help with any words. Read the poem again aloud and put in expression.

Make a list of the rhyming words:

_____   _____   _____

_____   _____   _____

_____   _____   _____

What is the poem is about?

_____

_____

_____

What do you like about the poem?

_____

_____

_____

The literacy work this week has been concerned with explanations. The children have:
- read a range of explanations which explain how or why something happens;
- written their own explanations using the key features of this type of writing.

What do you do between the time of getting up in the morning to arriving at school? Write an explanation of your morning routine on a separate sheet of paper.

You may want to think about using these features:

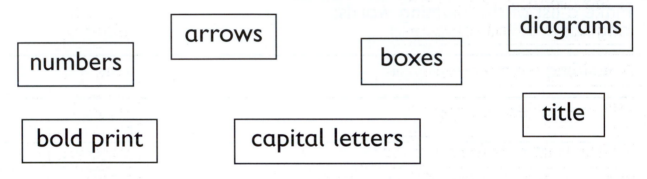

How will you begin your sentences? You may want to use some of these words and phrases:

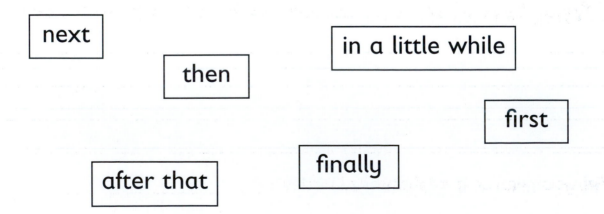

The literacy work this week has been concerned with dictionaries and other alphabetically ordered texts. The children have:
- found words in dictionaries using the first letter of a word.
- written their own dictionary definitions.
- learned to locate numbers in the phone book and Yellow Pages, using their knowledge of alphabetical order.

Match the word to its correct definition.

A sea creature with eight long arms called tentacles	plant
A building where people live	rain
When you feel unhappy	rope
Water that falls from clouds	octopus
Something which grows in the soil	sad
A piece of clothing which covers your foot	baby
A very young child	house
A piece of very thick string	sock

Can you think of five words and write definitions to go with them

_____

_____

_____

_____

Put your words in alphabetical order. _____

_____

_____

_____

The literacy work this week has been focused on books written by the same author. The children have:
- looked at a range of books, identifying the author and publisher;
- read a book by Martin Waddell and reviewed it thinking about settings, characters and themes.

Choose your favourite story book. This can be a book from school or home.

Write a review of this book using these headings. Write on a separate sheet of paper.

Title: _____

Author: _____

Publisher: _____

Characters: _____

_____

Setting: _____

_____

Theme: _____

_____

Favourite part: _____

_____

_____

_____

_____

Remember to give reasons for your opinions.

The literacy work this week has been concerned with comparing books written by the author Martin Waddell.
The children have:
• read two books by Martin Waddell and compared them thinking about settings, characters and themes.

Make a list of any books you have read which are written by the same author. Can you find any similarities between your chosen author's books?

Think about these things:
• Settings

• Characters

• Themes

• Illustrations

Who would you recommend your chosen author to? _____

_____

_____

_____

_____

Which is your favourite book by your chosen author? Why? _____

_____

_____

_____

_____

The literacy work this week has been focused on books written by the same author. The children have:
- read a range of books written by the author Martin Waddell
- reviewed a range of books by Martin Waddell identifying similarities and differences between them.
- considered other books that they know which are written by the same author.

Choose your favourite book by Martin Waddell. Write a blurb to the story which might go on the back of the book.

Remember to:
- describe the book briefly, giving an outline of the story;
- describe the theme;
- think about who you would recommend your book to.

The literacy work this week has been concerned with texts with language play with a focus on riddles.

The children have:

• read and discussed riddles;

• composed questions and answers about a chosen animal;

• used the answers to write a riddle about their animal.

Think of another animal, bird or insect and try to write a riddle by yourself or with help from an adult.

• make your riddle four lines long;

• write the title 'What am I?';

• think about what the creature looks like, what it eats, where it lives.

The literacy work this week is concerned with texts with language play and humorous verse.
The children have:
• discussed words and phrases in poems that create humour;
• read poems aloud with expression;
• written their own adaptations of poems.

At the end of the week we will be looking at tongue twisters and the use of alliteration (where adjacent and closely connected words begin with the same sound).

Either:
• Find a well known tongue twister from an appropriate poetry book; or
• Teach your child a tongue twister you already know; or
• Make up a range of alliterative phrases e.g. one wet wellington, several silent slithering snakes.

The literacy work this week has been concerned with two longer stories, one written in chapters.
The children have:
- listened to stories and told parts of the story in their own words.
- read about the author and written about themselves as authors.
- predicted what might happen next in one story.
- evaluated one story.

Someone has written this information about an author, but they have not quite got it right. Read through and correct so that it makes sense.

John Brown is born in Wales in 1980. She went to a village school and start to write stories when he was ten years old. John now lived in London with his brother paul and their dog Bubble and Sophie. I teaches at a local primary school and read his stories to her class before sending them to the publisher. John likes to swimming at the nearby swimming pool and walk in the mountains when he goes home to visit his parents.

The literacy work this week has been concerned with story writing. The children have:
- planned their own stories based on the stories we have been reading in class;
- written their own stories during the week.

Using your story plan, explain your story to an adult or an older brother, sister or friend.

In the boxes below sketch ideas for illustrations to go with your story. Think of an illustration to go with the beginning, the middle and the end. You will use these sketches next week to prepare your story for presentation to other children.

The literacy work this week has been concerned with completing and presenting stories the children have written to a standard where they can be read by others. The children have:
- finished writing and composing their stories;
- re-presented some of the text;
- illustrated the story;
- provided a title and cover illustration;
- added their author details, written earlier, to the book.

- Take your book home and read it again to yourself.
- Read the story to an adult or an older brother or sister. Remember to use expression to make the story interesting.
- Tell that person how you made your book, starting with your story plan.

The literacy work this week has been concerned with information books. The children have:
• discussed and used the terms 'fact' and 'fiction';
• read a range of information books and looked for their key features;
• used the contents, index and glossary pages of an information book.

Find an information book at home.

Can you find these things?

| Contents page |

| Index |

| Glossary |

| Sub-headings |

| Titles |

Find five facts in your book and write them down.

_____

_____

_____

_____

Which was the most interesting section in your book?

_____

_____

_____

The literacy work this week has been concerned with writing information texts. The children have:
- brainstormed questions they wish to answer during their reading;
- used a range of 'wh' words which can be used to begin questions;
- written their own pieces of information writing, using books they have read as examples.

Add the correct 'wh' word to the beginning of these questions.

what	when	which	where	who	why

1 do you live?

2 time do you get up in the mornings?

3 is your best friend?

4 type of crisp do you prefer?

5 do you like that flavour?

6 is your favourite book?

7 is your favourite pop group?

Try to answer these questions.

Can you think of some more questions beginning with these words. Make sure you spell them correctly!

Notes

Notes